Brian O'Kill

EXIT LINES

Famous (and not-so-famous)
Last Words

Longman

Longman Group Limited,
Longman House, Burnt Mill, Harlow,
Essex CM20 2JE, England
and Associated Companies throughout the world.

© Longman Group Limited 1986
All rights reserved; no part of this publication
may be reproduced, stored in a retrieval system,
or transmitted in any form or by any means, electronic,
mechanical, photocopying, recording, or otherwise,
without the prior written permission of the Publishers.

First published 1986

British Library Cataloguing in Publication Data

Exit Lines
1. Last words
I. O'Kill, Brian
080   PN6328.L3

ISBN 0-582-89223-6

Set in Linotron Optima and Century Schoolbook
by MCL Dataset Ltd.

Printed in Great Britain
by Mackays of Chatham, Kent.

ECC/USF LEARNING RESOURCES
8099 College Parkway, S.W.
P. O. Box 06210
Fort Myers, FL 33906-6210

Contents

Introduction	v
Addison, Joseph	1
Agatha, Saint	3
Augustus	4
Austen, Jane	6
Beethoven, Ludwig van	8
Brahe, Tycho	10
Buckingham, George Villiers, 1st Duke of	12
Buddha	17
Budgell, Eustace	19
Burns, Robert	20
Caesar, Julius	21
Caligula	23
Carew, Sir George	24
Caroline of Ansbach	26
Cavell, Edith	30
Charles II, King	32
Chekhov, Anton	34
Chesterfield, Philip Dormer Stanhope, 4th Earl of	35
Chopin, Frédéric	37
Corbet, Richard	39
Cranmer, Thomas	40
Crazy Horse	42
Descartes, René	44
Dickinson, Emily	46
Diderot, Denis	48
Digby, Sir Everard	50
Disraeli, Benjamin, 1st Earl of Beaconsfield	51
Duncan, Isadora	52
Elwes, John	53
Fairbanks, Douglas	55
Gainsborough, Thomas	56
George V, King	58
Godolphin, Sidney	59
Goethe, Johann Wolfgang von	61
Goffe, Thomas	63
Gogol, Nikolai	64
Goldsmith, Oliver	66
Green, Roosevelt	69
Grenville, Sir Richard	70
Hadrian	72
Hale, Nathan	74
Heine, Heinrich	76
Heylyn, Peter	78
Himmler, Heinrich	79
Hobbes, Thomas	81
Hopkins, Gerard Manley	83
Housman, A. E.	84
Ibsen, Henrik	86
Jackson, Thomas Jonathan ('Stonewall')	87

James, Henry	89
Jesus Christ	90
Johnson, Samuel	92
Judas Iscariot	94
Keats, John	95
Kelly, Ned	97
Latimer, Hugh	99
Laurel, Stan	101
Lawrence, Saint	103
Lennon, John	104
Mary I, Queen	105
Molière	107
Monmouth, James Scott, Duke of	109
Moore, Sir John	111
Mozart, Wolfgang Amadeus	114
Muhammad	116
Napoleon I	117
Nelson, Horatio, Viscount	120
Nero	122
Newton, Sir Isaac	124
Oates, Lawrence	126
Parnell, Charles Stewart	127
Pavlova, Anna	129
Perceval, Spencer	130
Pericles	131
Pheidippides	133
Picasso, Pablo	135
Pitt, William	136
Poe, Edgar Allan	139
Pompey	140
Pope, Alexander	142
Rabelais, François	144
Rasputin, Grigori Efimovich	146
Rhodes, Cecil	148
Richelieu, Armand-Jean du Plessis de	150
Roland, Marie-Jeanne	152
Sacco, Nicola and **Vanzetti**, Bartolomeo	154
Samson	156
Saul	157
Scott, Robert Falcon	159
Socrates	160
Stein, Gertrude	162
Stephen, Saint	163
Sterne, Laurence	164
Svevo, Italo	167
Taki, Zenzaburo	168
Thoreau, Henry David	171
Thurber, James	173
Vespasian	174
Wagner, Richard	176
Webern, Anton von	177
Select Bibliography	179

Introduction

This is a collection of accounts of various ways in which people have died and the words they have spoken at the end. It is not intended as a morbid tale of graves, of worms, and epitaphs, nor as a solemn treatise on the mysteries of death, nor as a sniggering joke. Rather, it presents episodes from the play of life which reveal a kaleidoscope of human attitudes and dilemmas. The cast includes saints, sinners, monarchs, politicians, soldiers, sailors, artists, musicians, and a miser; the scene shifts between six continents; the time covered is more than two millennia. It is by turns a tragedy and a comedy, a heroic drama and a farce; for in our last moments we can be, as we have been in our lives, sublime, pious, heroic, obscure, witty, odd, ludicrous, or – most probably – an enggrossing mixture of all these qualities.

Dying Voices

'*There is no subject I wish more to learn about*', wrote the French essayist Michel de Montaigne in the seventeenth century, '*than people's deaths: their words, appearance, and bearing at that point; there is no part of narratives to which I pay such attention.*' The widespread appeal of the subject has not depended merely on avid curiosity about intimate human details. In the first place, it is widely held – with some, although certainly not complete, justification – that one's manner of dying mirrors one's manner of living. It may be expected, at least, that a person's last message is an urgent, important, sincere statement: perhaps a deliberate summary of the achievements of a lifetime or the wisdom acquired during it, or perhaps a last-gasp confession or revelation. In addition, most major religions have adhered to belief in an afterlife – the notion that a soul or spirit survives the death of the body and continues to exist in some form, in some place. This usually leads to a conviction that people's final disposition determines their eternal fate; hence the final acts of life assume crucial importance. It may even be hoped that a person at the point of death may offer a glimpse of the next world, even though conventional conceptions of the afterlife suggest that it can be neither known nor expressed to the living.

Such expectations are both reflected and conditioned by literary treatments which have made us accustomed to 'famous last words' amounting to summary statements. Usually the reality is somewhat different – less articulate and portentous, but perhaps even more dramatic and revealing. However people try to prepare themselves for death, the act of dying may take them unawares and cut off the ability or desire to speak. Preparing in advance a dying speech may be a less-vain foible than composing one's own epitaph, but the occasion for delivering it can rarely be grasped (the case of Joseph Addison appears to be a notable exception). Doctors have reported that some patients who know themselves to be terminally ill have a fairly precise premonition of when they are going to die, but there are only two categories of people who can foreknow the exact hour of their death: suicides and victims of execution. Thanks to the traditions of the 'suicide note' and the formal last address often allowed to condemned people, both types are well represented in this book and offer a wide range of attitudes encompassing repentance, selfjustification, bravado, despair, and protestations of innocence.

Most final words, however, are spoken in ignorance of what is to come and are not intended as definitive statements. It is their unselfconscious, accidental, almost ironic quality which makes them so fascinating, so

v

richly human, and so amenable to whatever significance we may impute to them. They may form, unknowingly, a striking summary of a person's career and beliefs: Gertrude Stein's unanswerable last question or James Thurber's ambivalent final statement. Or they may seem to have a cryptic or symbolic quality which gives them a haunting resonance – as with Goethe's request for light, or the enigmatic words of 'Stonewall' Jackson.

Inevitably death will often catch people at a seemingly inappropriate time – when there is a curse, or a risqué joke, or a banal or careless remark, on their lips. Thus Denis Diderot died while arguing with his wife over an apricot, and Richard Wagner's last thought was of his watch. But whether these ends are really inappropriate may be doubted. Such moments are so characteristic of everyday lives, and so touchingly evocative of human frailty, that – although pious biographers have tended to disguise them – they surely do not belittle the people concerned.

This book illustrates a range of attitudes to death (corresponding, in general, to the distinct phases which doctors discern in fatally ill people). Anger and depression lie at one extreme, serene acceptance at the other. In between, there are moments when people deny the imminence of death – so producing ironically incongruous final assertions of their good health – or accept it stoically, or greet it with wry gallows humour (as in the case of Stan Laurel), or even mock it as Lytton Strachey did: *'If this is dying, I don't think much of it'*.

Most people are deeply afraid of death, but without analysing what there is to fear. The two main factors are surely loss and doubt. First, there is the absolute parting of the living from the dead: the dying person, suddenly isolated, may feel as bereaved as the survivors and in many instances (for example, Charles II and Nelson) seems to be principally concerned about their welfare. Secondly, there is the uncertainty of what lies beyond. There are really only two possibilities: either death is the end of all vital functions of the organism, or it leads to a new phase of eternal existence. Cicero perceived that the distinction might not even matter much: *'I shall either not be miserable, or I shall be happy'*. Admittedly, it is difficult to maintain this indifference, especially in the face of religious teaching that one's eternal life is blessed or damned in accordance with the final state of one's soul. It is not surprising that many final utterances concern religious matters – belief in and love of God, resignation to his will, repentance of sins, hope or confident expectation of a beatific afterlife – nor that doubt and disbelief sometimes seem to melt away in a deathbed conversion to religion (that of Heinrich Heine, for example). Even the most doubting person might be tempted to echo the ingenious double-barrelled prayer of a soldier before the battle of Blenheim in 1704: *'O God, if there be a God, save my soul, if I have a soul'*.

Reports and Rumours

Wonderful deathbed behaviour and sayings are commonly found in writings of the past. One may feel reluctant to spoil good stories, but when examining them critically, and attempting to trace them to a reliable source, one must conclude that a large number of them are false or inaccurate. The alleged final words seem either to have been fabricated, or modified – improved, bowdlerized, dramatized – or to have been a genuine utterance of the person concerned, but not to have been strictly a final speech.

Second-hand reports are rarely to be trusted, but even the testimony of eye-witnesses is often dubious, contradictory, or deficient. Death is usually a private business, attended by few witnesses; and they are not compellable, not bound by oath, and not necessarily competent. Even when well-intentioned, they are liable to the human failings of forgetfulness and inaccuracy – few of us are capable of repeating another person's words precisely – and incomprehension (when Albert Einstein died in Princeton in 1955 he spoke his last words in German – and nobody else in the room could understand a word of it).

One regrettable cause of falsification, still evident in popular writing, is the tendency to invest a statement with heightened importance by describing it as a person's last words. More damningly, it is clear that the reporting of a dying person's words has often involved undeclared interests – personal, political, religious, or moral. It may have been expedient to adduce evidence showing, for example, that an individual did or did not die in the Christian faith, or asserted innocence or guilt of a crime, or forgave or blamed enemies. If dying words are seen as the key to a person's life, there is an obvious temptation for a reporter to invent a suitable speech if none is available, to suppress one which seems inappropriate, or to polish a rough phrase.

It must also be borne in mind that biographical writing is usually swayed by the moral and artistic conventions of its time. Notions of accuracy, objectivity, and of what constitutes acceptable evidence have varied in different eras and cultures; so have notions of what is or is not fit to be made public. Assessing evidence from the past is rarely simple and, in attempting to delve beneath long-established legends about people's final words, I have often despaired of finding definitive information. What can one do when ultimately faced with silence, or improbability, or two variant accounts by the same witness, or wildly conflicting reports from different sources? From the available evidence it is impossible to decide whether William Pitt's last desire was for the welfare of his country or for a veal pie, and whether George V's final words enquired after his empire or profanely dismissed a seaside resort; if we have to make a choice between them, we can follow only our experience of human nature and history.

In any case, I do not believe that people's real or alleged final words can be properly appreciated out of context. Without attempting an inclusive account of any person's life, I have provided whatever information and explanatory comment seemed appropriate: not only details of the manner and circumstances of death, but also any relevant incidents and influences in the subjects' lives and an impression of their characters and attitudes. Often my method is unashamedly anecdotal, in that I have selected apparently trivial details in the belief that these often reveal more about people's natures than the accomplishments of their public careers. Vespasian being pelted with turnips, Sir Richard Grenville chewing glass, Goethe's absurd conversation with Heine, Ned Kelly in his homemade armour, Tycho Brahe's false nose – images of these things remain in the mind long after we have forgotten a mass of facts.

I remember vividly the choleric carbuncular face of the priest who aroused my interest in the subject of this book while I was at school. Among many educational anecdotes of his pastoral career, he told me of the occasion, many years before, when a pious wife had summoned him to the deathbed of her erring husband. Solemnly he painted the scene: his journey through a dark winter night, his youthful hopes of succouring and saving, his arrival in a dark room echoing with the laboured breaths of the dying man. He approached the bed, introduced himself in a whisper, and bent over to catch the final words forced out of the man's throat. 'He told me . . . he told me' – as I listened agog for a revelation, the priest himself seemed to find it hard to speak – 'he told me to bugger off.'

'And then', he added with selfjustifying relish, his face redder than ever, 'he died.' He paused, pouted, and drew the moral: 'As Shakespeare said,

As a tree falls, so shall it lie;
As a man lives, so shall he die.'

I was not quite convinced by the style or message of those two doggerel lines, which hardly measured up to Shakespeare even at his most leaden, but the story impressed me deeply. It evoked such perplexing mixed feelings of solemnity and irreverence, mystery and scandal, certitude and scepticism; and it reeked of truth and humanity. I have tried to allow those feelings to permeate this book.

Brian O'Kill

Notes on the Text

1. All texts from the Bible have been taken from the Authorized Version.

2. English texts written before the middle of the seventeenth century have been modernized in spelling and punctuation.

3. Foreign texts have been given in translation (my own, unless otherwise specified), apart from a few that are very familiar to English-speakers or virtually impossible to translate; these are given both in their original form and in English, as are speeches in a foreign language by English-speakers.

4. The adoption of the Gregorian or 'New Style' calendar at different times by different countries causes apparent discrepancies in dating which I have not tried to standardize. Thus the day of Anton Chekhov's death was 15 July in western Europe, but is generally (as here) referred to as 2 July, following the Russian reckoning.

Joseph
ADDISON
(1672–1719)

For, after a long and manly struggle with his distemper, he dismissed his physicians, and with them all hopes of life: but with his hope of life he dismissed not his concern for the living, but sent for a youth nearly related, and finely accomplished, yet not above being the better for good impressions from a dying friend. He came; but life now glimmering in the socket, the dying friend was silent. After a decent and proper pause, the youth said, 'Dear Sir! You sent for me: I believe, and I hope, that you have some commands; I shall hold them most sacred'. May distant ages not only hear, but feel, the reply! Forcibly grasping the youth's hand, he softly said, '**See in what peace a Christian can die**'. He spoke with difficulty, and soon expired.

Edward Young, *Conjectures on Original Composition* (1759)

Joseph Addison – man of letters and politician, best-known today for his essays in the periodicals *The Tatler* and *The Spectator* – addressed this famous valediction to his dissipated stepson, the Earl of Warwick. His death, occurring on 17 June 1719 at his home, Holland House in Kensington, followed a long period of declining health – severe asthma, later accompanied by dropsy – which had been adduced as the reason for his resignation from his position as Secretary of State in March 1718.

The authenticity of Young's narrative has been questioned by several writers, largely because it seems too neat and contrived. Although Young was not himself an eye-witness of Addison's death, he stated that he was given this account immediately after the event by Thomas Tickell (1686–1740), who had been Addison's literary and political protégé for a decade, and was present at his deathbed. (He edited Addison's works in 1721, appending a worthy elegy 'To the Earl of Warwick on the Death of Mr Addison'.) A more recent biographer, Peter Smithers, expresses no doubts of the narrative. He comments: 'The whole of Addison's life in its consistency pointed to such a studied ending. The words uttered would be sincere, and in keeping with all of Addison's teaching; and it is inconceivable that such a man, who had written so much on the subject of death, should not have prepared himself therefor'.

Addison may have been been influenced by an incident in January 1719. Sir Samuel Garth, a physician and poet, 'sent to Addison (of whom he had a very high opinion) on his deathbed, to ask him whether the Christian religion was true'. The writer of this story does not record Addison's answer, but mentions that Garth, although dying a Catholic, 'was rather doubtful, and fearful, than religious' (Joseph Spence, *Anecdotes, Observations, and Characters of Books and Men*).

A less tolerant view of Addison's behaviour has been taken by others. In a letter of 16 May 1759, Horace Walpole – rarely the most charitable of men – wickedly parodied Young's account with reference to the common rumour that the decay of Addison's health had been accelerated by intemperate habits: 'Unluckily he died of brandy – nothing makes a Christian die in peace like being maudlin [i.e. drunk]'.

Addison's writing on death had a fatal influence on his kinsman Eustace Budgell; see p. 19. His deathbed scene was re-enacted by the British soldier Sir Henry Havelock (1795–1857), who said to his son: **'See how a Christian can die!'**.

Saint
AGATHA
(died 251?)

Lord, you who created me, and protected me from my infancy, and made me act with courage in my youth; you who took away from me love of the world, kept my body free from pollution; who made me overcome the hangman's tortures, the sword, fire, and chains; who gave me the virtue of patience in the midst of tortures; I beg you to receive my soul now: for it is time that you order me to leave this world here, and to come to your mercy.

Acta Sanctorum, edited by J. Bollandus and G. Henschenius (February, Vol. I).

St Agatha was a beautiful Sicilian virgin, born of a noble family in either Catania or Palermo. She inadvertently inflamed the lust of a Roman administrator named Quintian who, having failed in his initial advances to her, exploited the laws against Christians in an effort to coerce her.

He sent her to a brothel, but she remained obdurate; he threatened her, but she would not yield; he had her beaten and stretched on the rack, but she was adamantly chaste. As a further punishment or coercion, her breasts were crushed and cut off. Thus it is that artistic representations of St Agatha often show her with her dismembered breasts on a dish. Curiously, in the Middle Ages this object was mistaken for a dish of loaves, giving rise to the practice of blessing bread on the saint's feast-day.

Thrown into prison without food or medical care, she was consoled by a vision of St Peter. But Quintian's patience was now at an end, and by his orders she was rolled naked over red-hot coals mixed with potsherds, whereupon she uttered the speech quoted above and died immediately.

So, with certain variations, say the accounts collected by two seventeenth-century Jesuits in the *Acta Sanctorum*, a vast compilation of materials in Latin relating to early Christian saints. Of the historical existence of St Agatha there is not a scrap of evidence. There is, indeed, hardly anything in the accounts which can be related to any known time or place; the traditional date of her death, 5 February 251, is altogether unsubstantiated. One can say only that the story is old, and that it may have some basis in reality. If we choose to disbelieve in these horrible events, we may be faced with an even more disturbing view of them as the sadistic fantasies of a pious pornographer. It is easy to say that such things never happen; but there is a remarkable modern parallel in the case of a Zairean nun, beatified by Pope John Paul II in 1985, who was beaten, bayoneted, and finally shot by rebel troops in 1964 after refusing to break her vow of chastity. Sister Anuarite M. Nengapeta, aged twenty-three, reportedly told the soldiers that she would die to protect her virginity, and uttered these last words: '**I forgive you because you know not what you do. It is thus that I would have it end**'. The soldier who killed her has become a devout recluse, and claims to have seen Sister Anuarite in visions.

AUGUSTUS
(63 BC–AD 14)

Livia, do not forget our marriage; farewell!
Suetonius, 'Augustus', *Lives of the Caesars* (written *ca* 120)

Gaius Octavius, great-nephew of Julius Caesar, was named in Caesar's will as his heir, and assumed the name Gaius Julius Caesar Octavianus. From 43–31 BC he was a member of the second triumvirate, along with Antony and Lepidus; after defeating Antony at Actium in 31 BC he became sole ruler of the Roman world, and in 27 BC the Roman senate

Augustus

gave him the name Augustus (i.e. sacred, venerable). After ruling for forty-five years as the first emperor of Rome, he died on 19 August 14 in his father's old home at Nola, near Naples. His corpse was carried solemnly to Rome and burned, and he was deified by the senate.

Augustus has frequently been credited with this final statement: '**Have I played my part satisfactorily in the farce of life?**'. Although the biographer Suetonius records this, he clearly states that his final words – spoken almost immediately before he died – were those quoted above.

Augustus addressed his farewell to his wife, Livia Drusilla (known as Julia Augusta after his death), to whom he had been married for fifty-two years. Yet it did not commemorate a completely devoted, blameless union; one may wonder, indeed, whether there was some ironic or cryptic purport in his words. Augustus had been twice previously married: to Claudia, Mark Antony's stepdaughter, and to Scribonia, both of whom he divorced. According to Suetonius, he then took Livia from her husband, Claudius Tiberius Nero, although she was pregnant at the time. Moreover, he was notoriously a womanizer and allegedly fond of men as well ('we may remark', notes Edward Gibbon, 'that of the first fifteen emperors Claudius was the only one whose taste in love was entirely correct').

Suetonius makes no suggestion that Augustus's death was due to anything other than natural causes. But the historian Tacitus (*Annals*, Bk I), writing at about the same time, reports that in some quarters his wife was suspected of foul play; anxious to ensure the succession of her son Tiberius, she was concerned over Augustus's growing favour towards Agrippa Postumus, his grandson. In the event, Tiberius succeeded Augustus but quarrelled with his mother, accusing her of meddling in the government, and refused even to attend her funeral. That Augustus's death should attract some suspicion is scarcely surprising, for of his ten successors only Vespasian (see p. 174) and Titus definitely died naturally. Gaius (Caligula; see p. 23), Galba, Vitellius, and Domitian were all murdered; Nero (see p. 122) and Otho killed themselves under duress; Tiberius and Claudius were, according to rumour, poisoned.

Jane
AUSTEN
(1775–1817)

She supported, during two months, all the varying pain, irksomeness, and tedium, attendant on decaying nature, with more than resignation, with a truly elastic cheerfulness. She retained her faculties, her memory, her fancy, her temper, and her affections, warm, clear, and unimpaired, to the last.... Her last voluntary speech conveyed thanks to her medical attendant; and to the final question asked of her, purporting to know her wants, she replied, '**I want nothing but death**'.

> from the anonymous 'Biographical Notice of the Author' [by Henry Austen] prefixed to Jane Austen's *Northanger Abbey* (1818)

Jane Austen died in Winchester – where she had moved in May 1817 to seek medical advice – early in the morning of 18 July 1817, and was buried in Winchester Cathedral. Her family could explain the cause of her death only as 'a decay, deep and incurable', and several later biographers have been puzzled by the illness which manifested itself at the beginning of 1816. A modern physician has plausibly diagnosed the fatal condition as Addison's disease, a chronic disorder of the adrenal glands, which was not identified until the middle of the nineteenth century.

The account quoted above was written by Jane Austen's favourite brother, Henry, who became a clergyman in 1816 shortly after being bankrupted by the collapse of a banking business in which he was involved. A letter from her sister, Cassandra (1773–1845), adds some further details of her last moments:

> She felt herself to be dying about half an hour before she became tranquil and apparently unconscious. During that half-hour was her struggle, poor soul! She said she could not tell us what she suffered, though she complained of little fixed pain. When I asked her if there was anything she wanted, her answer was she wanted nothing but death, and some of her words were: '**God grant me patience, pray for me, oh, pray for me!**' Her voice was affected, but as long as she spoke she was intelligible.

Although death rarely impinges upon the largely placid world of Jane Austen's novels, her life was by no means sheltered from it. Even if we disregard the unsubstantiated popular story of the death of a man she loved, we know that she was affected by the death in 1797 of Cassandra's fiancé, the deaths in riding accidents of a cousin and a close friend, and the sudden death of her father in 1805. It was on this last occasion that she wrote to her brother Frank in terms which uncannily prefigure her own final wish:

> When we understood his recovery to be hopeless, most fervently did we pray for the speedy release which ensued. To have seen him languishing long, struggling for hours, would have been dreadful, and, thank God, we were all spared from it.

Ludwig van
BEETHOVEN
(1770–1827)

Pity, pity – too late!
A. W. Thayer, *The Life of Ludwig van Beethoven*, edited by H. E. Krehbiel (1921)

Beethoven's final illness was protracted and painful. It began as soon as he returned to Vienna at the beginning of December 1826 after visiting his brother in the country, and from that time he was confined to his room. Dropsy was the obvious symptom, but retrospective diagnosis indicates that the underlying cause was cirrhosis of the liver. Totally deaf, agonizingly swollen by fluid, worried about money and the wayward behaviour of his nephew and ward Karl, more suspicious and cantankerous than ever, attended by too many doctors prescribing different and useless treatments – in this condition Beethoven lingered on for nearly four months. He died on the afternoon of 26 March 1827, to the accompaniment of a thunderstorm.

Details of the last phase of the composer's life are recorded by a number of witnesses. Unfortunately self-contradictions and discrepancies between them are evident. Nor has the situation been improved by later embroideries, such as the seemingly baseless attribution to Beethoven of the final words '**I shall hear in heaven**'. However, there is general agreement about three of his latest utterances.

On 23 March Beethoven said: '**Plaudite, amici, comoedia finita est**' ['**Applaud, friends, the comedy is over**'], the Latin phrase supposedly uttered by an actor at the end of a Roman comedy. The idea expressed here is almost a commonplace (see entry on Rabelais, p. 144), yet the occasion of its utterance is controversial. Two reports state that the composer spoke these words almost immediately after receiving the last rites – 'in his favourite sarcastic-humorous manner', wrote one witness – and the notion that Beethoven was referring to the sacrament in this way caused some scandal. It now seems almost certain, however, that Beethoven made this remark after speaking to his doctors, and that the sacrament was not administered until 24 March.

On the morning of 24 March Beethoven exclaimed '**God bless them!**' – 'them' being the people of England, and the cause of his gratitude a loan of £100 from the Philharmonic Society of London. When the Society, which had enthusiastically embraced the cause of Beethoven's music, heard in February that he was ill and in financial straits, the directors immediately voted to give him an advance on a benefit concert they were planning to hold, and the money reached Vienna on 15 March. It must be said, however, that Beethoven's supposed impoverishment, which he himself publicized, was more apparent than real; he had a fair sum of money hidden away, but was unshakably resolved to keep this as a legacy for his nephew.

One of Beethoven's doctors had recommended that he should drink good Rhine wine to relieve his illness. Finding this commodity impossible to obtain in Vienna, he had written to his publishers, Schott and Sons in Mainz, to ask them to send him some. They sent him twelve bottles, and on their own initiative added a further consignment of two bottles of wine and two of wine mixed with herbs. But delivery was slow, and Beethoven wrote two further importunate letters: '**My health, which will not be restored for a long time, pleads for the wines which I have asked for and which will certainly bring me refreshment, strength and health**'. The wine eventually arrived at 1 p.m. on 24 March. On seeing it, Beethoven murmured '**Pity, pity – too late!**'. A few spoonfuls of the wine were given to him during the afternoon, but he lost consciousness later that day and remained in his death-throes for forty-eight hours.

Detractors of Beethoven have used this final reference to wine, together with the cause of his death, to uphold rumours that he habitually drank to excess. This is grossly unjust, for reliable evidence suggests that Beethoven was an abstemious man; the Dionysiac element in his character and work was innate and needed no external stimulus. It is noteworthy, however, that his last words introduce what might be called the wine *motif*, which reappears at the deaths of Chekhov (see p. 34) and Johannes Brahms, among others. According to some accounts, on the night before his death Brahms took a glass of wine and said '**Ah, that tastes good, thank you**'. In view of the fact that Brahms constantly felt himself overshadowed by his mighty predecessor and has been unfairly criticized as an imitator of Beethoven, it is particularly ironic that he should have echoed Beethoven at this point.

Tycho
BRAHE
(1546–1601)

Let me not seem to have lived in vain!
account by Johann Kepler, quoted by J. L. E. Dreyer, *Tycho Brahe* (1890), and J. A. Gade, *The Life and Times of Tycho Brahe* (1947)

The modern study of planetary astronomy has its origin in the work of Tycho Brahe, despite the fact that his cosmology was basically erroneous. Born under Danish rule, in a region that is now part of Sweden, Brahe began serious astronomic investigations in his mid-twenties, and studied for twenty years in a special observatory established under royal patronage before moving to Prague, at the invitation of the emperor Rudolf II, in 1599. Without the aid of telescopes, he discovered an important new star in the constellation of Cassiopeia, established the variations of the moon, recorded the positions of the stars and planets, and corrected the known values of many astronomical quantities. It was from Brahe's observations, considerably more accurate than those previously accepted, that his German pupil Johann Kepler deduced the three laws of planetary motion which in turn formed the basis of Newtonian astronomy.

Brahe's own deductions about the structure of the solar system were, however, some way wide of the mark. The second-century astronomer Ptolemy wrote that the sun, planets, and stars revolved round the earth – an idea that was unquestioned for nearly fifteen hundred years, until Nicolaus Copernicus (1473–1543) argued that the earth and planets revolved round the sun. Brahe's notion was a curious blend of the geocentric (Ptolemaic) and heliocentric (Copernican) systems: he believed that the five known planets orbited the sun, but that the sun, planets, and stars all orbited the earth. In this conclusion Brahe at least overcame some of the contradictions in Copernicus's argument, and he was still in advance of his time – most of his work was done before that of Galileo Galilei (1564–1642), who in 1633 was compelled by the Church to recant his belief in the Copernican system. It was the news of Galileo's condemnation which dissuaded René Descartes (see p. 44) from publishing his own completed work in support of this dangerously heterodox theory. Descartes ultimately circumvented the problem by a fantastic equivocation: he argued that although the earth goes round the sun, it does not actually *move* but is carried in a vortex.

Brahe died in Prague on 24 October 1601, after eleven days of illness. He had suffered from a recurrent bladder problem, and reportedly aggravated the condition by drinking copiously at a dinner party without venturing to leave the table to relieve himself. Kepler, who had joined him in Prague the previous year, wrote a brief account of his death, from which the words quoted above are taken (whether Brahe actually spoke in Latin, the language in which Kepler wrote, we cannot tell). In delirium on the night before his death, Kepler reported, 'he frequently repeated these words, as if he were composing a poem'. Other accounts, however, indicate that these were not strictly Brahe's last words, since in the morning he recovered sufficiently to enjoin his younger son to continue studying, to beg Kepler to complete the astronomical tables on which they were working, and to thank a friend for his kindness.

One further peculiarity of Brahe deserves mention. In 1566 he had most of his nose cut off in a duel, mainly caused by a quarrel about mathematics. He had an artificial nose made of gold and silver, and always carried with him a small pot of glue so that he could fasten the contraption if it came loose. It has been suggested that this disfigurement was responsible for his unsuitable marriage to a peasant girl; he may have felt himself incapable of winning the affection of a woman who was his social equal.

George Villiers, 1st Duke of BUCKINGHAM
(1592–1628)

(a) This day betwixt nine and ten of the clock in the morning, the Duke of Buckingham then coming out of a Parlour into a Hall, to go to his coach and so to the King . . . was by one Felton (once a Lieutenant of this our Army) slain at one blow, with a dagger-knife. In his staggering he turn'd about, uttering only this word, '**Villain!**' & never spake word more, but presently plucking out the knife from himself, before he fell to the ground, he made towards the Traitor, two or three paces, and then fell against a Table.

Dudley Carleton, letter to Queen Henrietta Maria, 23 August 1628

(b) After breakfast the Duke going out, Colonel Fryer stept before him, and stopped him upon some business, and Lieutenant Felton, being behind, made a thrust with a common tenpenny knife over Fryer's arm at the Duke, which lighted so fatally that he slit his heart in two, leaving the knife sticking in the body. The Duke took out the knife and threw it away; and laying his hand on his sword, and drawing it half out, said, '**The villain hath killed me**' . . . so reeling against a chimney, he fell down dead.

James Howell, letter to Lady Scroop, 25 August 1628

(c) The Duke was stabbed some 2 foot within the parlour, going into the hall, his horse being at the door ready for him to go to the Court. He was slain by a stroke of a knife in the left pap, about 9 in the morning. Felton stood in the parlour next to the street and stabbed the Duke with a back-blow over Fryer's shoulder . . . The Duke uttered no more words but '**Zounds, villain**', and, himself, plucking out the knife, went 3 steps into the hall, thinking to have killed him with that knife, but fainted and fell down by the clock there.

from the commonplace book of Sir John Oglander (printed in *A Royalist's Notebook*, edited by F. Bamford, 1936)

(d) In that very Passage, turning himself to speak with Sir Thomas Fryar, a Colonel of the Army, who was then speaking near his ear, he was on the suddain struck over his shoulder upon the Breast with a Knife; upon which, without using any other words, but, '**The Villain hath kill'd me**'; and in the same moment pulling out the Knife himself, he fell down dead, the Knife having pierced his heart.

Edward Hyde, Lord Clarendon, *The True Historical Narrative of the Rebellion and the Civil Wars in England*, Book I (1702)

THESIS

Alien they seemed to be:
No mortal eye could see
The intimate welding of their later history

Thomas Hardy, *The Convergence of the Twain.*

George Villiers: third son of the impoverished Sir George Villiers, and a family 'rather without obscurity than with any great lustre', according to Sir Henry Wotton's *Reliquiae Wottonianae* (1651). He was an undistinguished but effeminately handsome youth when he was introduced to King James I in August 1614. The King's attention – more than his attention – was attracted, and he made Villiers his Cupbearer. From then on, he prospered spectacularly: 'Never any man, in any age', wrote Lord Clarendon, 'nor, I believe, in any country or nation, rose, in so short a time, to so much greatness of honour, fame, and fortune, upon no other advantage or recommendation than of the beauty and gracefulness and becomingness of his person'.

In April 1615 Villiers was knighted and made, more or less appropriately, Gentleman of the King's Bedchamber; in January 1616 he became Master of the King's Horse, despite having learned to ride only in the previous month; in August 1616 he was created Viscount Villiers; in January 1617 he was elevated to Earl of Buckingham, and was made a privy councillor a month later; in January 1618 he became Marquis of Buckingham; in January 1619, Lord High Admiral; in May 1623, Earl of Coventry and Duke of Buckingham. That is not to mention numerous other honours heaped on him by the doting monarch – 'in dispensing whereof', Clarendon noted, 'he was guided more by the rules of appetite than of judgment'. James nicknamed his favourite 'Steenie', for his alleged resemblance to the angelic face of St Stephen; in letters to the King, Villiers signed himself 'Your majesty's most humble slave and dog'.

Now one of the wealthiest men in England, and virtual ruler of the country, Buckingham retained his influence after the death of James in 1625. But his bungling, and consequent unpopularity, also continued. In October of that year he was responsible for a vast expedition to attack the Spanish port of Cadiz. The venture – in which Buckingham himself did not take part – was so woefully organized and equipped that it accomplished nothing but the loss of ships and men; yet when Parliament introduced a bill in May 1626 to impeach him for this disaster, King Charles simply dissolved Parliament to halt the proceedings. There was a further setback in the following year, when Buckingham led an unsuccessful expedition to relieve La Rochelle, the Huguenot garrison in France which was under siege by the French government. On this occasion Buckingham at least showed personal bravery, although his tactics deserved little praise. Nevertheless, a further expedition to La Rochelle was planned in 1628, and on 17 August Buckingham came to Portsmouth to organize it. Soon after he arrived, three hundred sailors surrounded his coach, asking for the pay that was due to them. Buckingham had the ringleader arrested and swiftly condemned to death. When the man's colleagues staged a demonstration against this decision, Buckingham and his followers charged at them on horseback with drawn swords, killing two sailors and wounding many others; he then personally supervised the execution of the condemned man.

ANTITHESIS
Or signs that they were bent
By paths coincident
On being anon twin halves of one august event

John Felton: born about 1595, of an old Suffolk family, and 'by nature of a deep melancholy, silent, and gloomy constitution, but bred in the active way of a soldier', according to Wotton. Felton served as a lieutenant at Cadiz and La Rochelle, was wounded, and lost the use of his left arm. His expected promotion to captain was blocked – perhaps because he had quarrelled with one of Buckingham's protégés – and his pay was in arrears. When he complained to Buckingham in 1627 about this situation, he was told that he could go and hang himself; and so, indirectly, he did.

Felton had evidently brooded over the injustices of worldly success before he set out, on 19 August 1628, from London for Portsmouth. It was not merely revenge for his own wrongs that filled his mind, but a belief that he had a mission to free his country from the man whose misdeeds had been so clearly expounded in the remonstrance passed by Parliament. He had bought a cheap strong knife on Tower Hill, prayed in a church in Fleet Street, and in the lining of his hat he had sewn two messages, stating 'He is unworthy of the name of a Gentleman, or Soldier, in my opinion, that is afraid to sacrifice his life for the honour of God, his King, and Country' (the exact wording differs in various accounts, although all express the same idea).

SYNTHESIS

*Till the Spinner of the Years
Said 'Now!' And each one hears,
And consummation comes –*

The two men finally drew together on the morning of 23 August 1628, at the house of Captain Robert Mason in High Street, Portsmouth, where Buckingham was lodging. There Felton, immediately after his arrival in the town, stabbed him to death. In the confusion that followed, the assassin might easily have escaped; but, perhaps overcome by emotion or, more probably, accepting that his role was played out, he stayed on the scene, betrayed himself, and was arrested. When he was brought to London on 11 September, crowds gathered to congratulate him on delivering England from an oppressor. He pleaded guilty at his trial, claiming that his act had been for the good of his country, and was hanged at Tyburn on 29 November.

Of the writers of the four accounts of Buckingham's death quoted above, Carleton was an eye-witness of the event; Howell and Oglander state that they received reports from eye-witnesses; and Clarendon, although not a witness and writing twenty years later, was the premier historian of that time and might be expected to produce a definitive version. It is noteworthy that, although all give similar accounts of Buckingham's death, they differ in several details, and only two of them agree precisely on his last words.

BUDDHA
(563?–483? BC)

Now then, monks, I address you; subject to decay are compound things: strive with earnestness.
from the *Mahāparinibbāna-sutta*
('The Book of the Great Decease'), quoted by Edward J. Thomas,
The Life of Buddha as Legend and History (1927)

Few modern scholars doubt – as their predecessors did – that the Buddha was a historical personage, yet the traditional narratives of his life are so varied and mingled with dubious or legendary elements that it is difficult to derive a coherent and uncontroversial biography. Different schools of Buddhism throughout the East have produced separate accounts, whose sources and chronology are hopelessly confused. Probably the oldest of these, and the ones most used by western scholars, are the scriptures of the Theravāda school, written in the Indic language Pāli.

According to the Pāli writings, the Buddha was the son of the king of the Sakyas, probably inhabiting a region on the borders of India and Nepal. His family name was Gautama (in Sanskrit) or Gotama (in Pāli); his given name was Siddhārtha, meaning 'one whose aim is accomplished'. Buddha was not his individual name, but a title meaning 'the enlightened one'; Buddhists believe that there were at least six buddhas before Gautama, and there will be further ones in the future. Among many other titles given to the Buddha, the most common are Sākyamuni ('the sage from the Sakya tribe'), Bhagavā ('Lord'), and Tathāgata ('He who has thus come').

He led the indolent existence of a princeling until the age of twenty-nine, when, becoming aware of pain, disease, and death, he renounced his luxurious mode of life and became a wandering ascetic. Six years later he attained enlightenment (bodhi), and for the rest of his days, which are sparsely documented, he travelled, preached, and won disciples.

Buddha

The most notable source of information about the Buddha's last days is the *Mahāparinibbāna-sutta*, a canonical Pāli text interspersing biographical material with discourses by the Buddha. It tells how the Buddha, at the age of eighty, travelled north and arrived in May at Kusinārā (now Kasia) in northeast India. Lying on his right side in a park, he prepared to attain nirvana (the annihilation of craving and selfhood). After addressing his chief disciple, Ānanda, three times he asked his followers whether they had any doubts or queries which they wished him to resolve. Since they all remained silent, he finally spoke to them the words quoted above, which he had also uttered three months before his death: his final message of the need to renounce transient earthly things ('compound things', a phrase which has also been translated as 'all conditioned things', 'all component things', and 'all things that come into being') and seek the light.

He then passed into a series of trances, losing consciousness and feeling, and attained nirvana. Frightful thunder and a great earthquake followed his death; Ashvaghosha's *Buddhacarita*, a poetic biography written in the first or second century AD, adds that darkness spread over the earth, rivers filled with boiling water, and unseasonal flowers fell onto his body from the trees beneath which he lay.

Eustace
BUDGELL
(1686–1737)

**What Cato did, and Addison approved,
Cannot be wrong.**

In his death, as in his life, Eustace Budgell remained under the influence of his cousin, Joseph Addison (see p. 1).

Born near Exeter, educated at Oxford, and subsequently called to the Bar, Budgell was taken to Ireland in 1710 by Addison – then secretary to the Lord-Lieutenant of Ireland – as one of his clerks. After this, he shared Addison's lodgings in London and contributed essays to Addison's periodical, *The Spectator*. In 1717, through Addison's influence, he was appointed Accountant-General of Ireland, but soon lost the position as a consequence of lampooning the new Lord-Lieutenant's secretary. In 1720 he lost £20,000 by investing in the 'South Sea Bubble'. His mind apparently became somewhat unhinged and, although continuing to write reasonable essays and verse, he involved himself in a number of vexatious lawsuits and published several pamphlets detailing his grievances. Eventually he fell under suspicion of forging a bequest to himself in the will of Matthew Tindal, a controversial theologian who died in 1733. On 4 May 1737 Budgell filled his pockets with stones, took a boat on the Thames, jumped out into the river, and drowned himself.

On Budgell's desk was found a piece of paper bearing the line-and-a-half of verse quoted above – a movingly brief justification of suicide. The Roman statesman Cato the Younger (Marcus Porcius Cato, 95–46 BC) stabbed himself, rather than surrender, after joining Pompey's unsuccessful struggle against Julius Caesar; his alleged last words were **'Now I am master of myself'**. Addison presented this event in his frigid play *Cato*; here Cato, just before killing himself,

Budgell

meditates on the glorious immortality of the soul and expresses his determination to
>   get loose
> From this vain world, th'abode of guilt and sorrow.

Robert
BURNS
(1759–1796)

John, don't let the awkward squad fire over me.
Allan Cunningham, 'Life of Burns', in
The Works of Robert Burns (1834)

The funeral of Robert Burns took place in Dumfries on 25 July 1796. Despite the rainy weather, a crowd of as many as 12,000 people accompanied the poet's body to St Michael's kirkyard. As a member of the Royal Dumfries Volunteers, Burns was buried with military honours; and as his coffin was lowered into the grave, three ragged volleys were fired.

This last circumstance was precisely what Burns deprecated when he addressed his last recorded words to a fellow-member of the Volunteers. He was not by nature a military man, and feared the unseemly havoc which could be wrought by untrained recruits (the 'awkward squad'). The whole story of his connection with the volunteers is an odd one. Originally he had been an ardent supporter of the French revolution, expressing his sympathies so incautiously that he lost a chance of promotion in his work as an excise officer. But in 1795, when a French invasion of Britain was threatened, patriotism – perhaps mingled with prudence – led him to change his views. He helped to organize the Dumfries Volunteers, and commemorated them in stirring verses:

> Does haughty Gaul invasion threat?
> Then let the louns [i.e. fellows] beware, Sir;

> There's wooden walls upon our seas,
> And volunteers on shore, Sir.

Burns's health had been in decline since the beginning of 1796, a result of rheumatic fever allegedly exacerbated by a chill caught while he was returning home late after a convivial night at the Globe tavern. By April his condition was so bad that he wrote 'I close my eyes in misery and open them without hope'. At the beginning of July he greeted a female visitor with the striking words: 'Well, madam, have you any commands for the other world?'. His final days were further depressed by poverty and anxiety about the fate of his wife and four young children. A visit to the sea failed to improve him, and he died on 21 July after three days of delirium.

During the funeral his wife, Jean Armour, gave birth to a son, who died shortly afterwards. Thanks to an appeal fund, however, the poet's family were well provided for after his death.

Gaius Julius
CAESAR
(100–44 BC)

(a) **You too, my child?**
Suetonius, 'Caesar', *Lives of the Caesars* (written *ca* 120)

(b) **You villain, Casca, what are you doing?**
Plutarch, *Life of Caesar* (written *ca* 120)

(c) **Et tu, Brute?** [**You too, Brutus?**]
traditional

Gaius Julius Caesar was assassinated at a meeting of the Roman senate on 15 March 44 BC. His dictatorial powers, his arrogance, and his apparent aspirations to monarchy and divinity, had roused widespread fear and resentment among both plebeians and patricians. A group of some sixty conspirators, led by Gaius Cassius Longinus and Marcus Junius Brutus, planned and carried out his murder.

The two early detailed accounts of his death, by Suetonius and Plutarch, agree in outline but not on all points; both writers, moreover, confess that there are alternative versions of events.

According to Suetonius, the first dagger-blow was struck by Casca, a Tribune of the People, or by his brother. It wounded Caesar in the neck, but only slightly. He, in return, stabbed Casca in the arm – but then another blow struck him and, resigning himself to his fate, he drew the top of his toga over his face and stood there while he was stabbed twenty-three times. One report says that he did not utter a word; another states that, when he saw Brutus about to strike him, he reproached him in Greek with the words quoted in (a) above. This phrase 'my child' (which could also be translated as 'my son') has two possible interpretations. Probably it simply reflects the fact that Brutus was Caesar's protégé; after siding with Pompey against Caesar in the civil war of 49-48 BC, Brutus had been pardoned by Caesar and received honours and favours from him. But there was a rumour – unlikely enough, although incapable of absolute refutation – that Brutus was Caesar's illegitimate son, and it could be argued that Caesar, in his extremity, acknowledged this.

Plutarch, however, tells that Caesar cried out in Latin – the words quoted in (b) above – when Casca struck the first blow. Some say, Plutarch reports, that Caesar fought against the assassins until he saw that Brutus was among them; then he covered his head and sank to the ground (see also entry on Pompey, p. 140).

The traditional version (c) of Caesar's last words has been current at least since the late sixteenth century. It is familiar from its use in Shakespeare's *Julius Caesar* (probably written in 1599), where Caesar's last cry is 'Et tu, Brute? – Then fall Caesar!', although this is not its first known appearance. It occurs in an earlier play, *The True Tragedie of Richard Duke of York* (published in 1595), considered by most modern critics to be an abridged and corrupted version of Shakespeare's *Henry VI Part 3*, but sometimes taken to be either an early version of that play or an anonymous work on which it was based. Whether or not Shakespeare himself originated the phrase is unknown; certainly it is not found in this form in any classical source, although one must assume it to be a reworking of the Greek words quoted by Suetonius.

CALIGULA
(12–41)

> As he lay writhing, shouting **'I am still alive!'**, the others finished him off with thirty wounds.
> Suetonius, 'Gaius', *Lives of the Caesars* (written *ca* 120)

Gaius Caesar, son of the Roman general Germanicus, was nicknamed Caligula ('Little Boot') on account of the military boots he wore while growing up in his father's camp. Becoming Emperor in 37 on the death of his great-uncle Tiberius – whom, according to rumours, he poisoned or strangled – Caligula was initially popular and ruled decently for about eight months. Then, probably deranged as a consequence of a severe illness – although he had already revealed in private his viciousness and perversion – he gave rein to capricious despotism, violence, and immorality. He committed incest with each of his three sisters, and took whatever women – not to mention men – he wanted; devised extraordinary extravagances in eating, drinking, and other amusements; passed the most absurd regulations; staged revoltingly bloodthirsty shows; condemned people to torture or death for the most trifling offences; prayed for a great catastrophe to make his reign memorable; wished that the Roman people had only one neck so that he could kill them all at a single stroke; and always cheated when playing dice.

Caligula was murdered just after noon on 25 January 41, by a group of conspirators led by Cassius Chaerea, a senior officer in the imperial bodyguard. Quite apart from any political motive, Cassius hated the Emperor for mocking his effeminacy and making obscene gestures at him in public. The biographer Suetonius records two variant accounts of Caligula's death. In one, Cassius wounded him in the neck and another soldier finished him off by stabbing him in the breast. In another, Cassius split the Emperor's jawbone with a blow; but Caligula, on the ground, shouted '**I am still alive!**' before he died from thirty further wounds inflicted by a number of assassins.

Sir George CAREW

(died 1545)

I have a sort of knaves whom I cannot rule.
John Hooker (alias Vowell), 'The discourse and discovery of the life of Sir Peter Carew', printed as *The Life and Times of Sir Peter Carew, Kt*, edited by John Maclean (1857)

On 19 July 1545 the south coast of England was threatened by a large fleet sent by King Francis I of France. The English fleet mustered in Portsmouth harbour, where Henry VIII dined on board the admiral's flagship. Also present at the meal was the vice-admiral, Sir George Carew, to whom the King gave a chain from around his own neck, together with many encouraging words.

Carew's ship, the *Mary Rose*, was one of the prides of the navy: 700 tons, carrying 90 guns and, on this occasion, an enlarged complement of 700 men. Carew himself was a soldier of considerable reputation, who had served as Lieutenant-General of the Horse in the campaign against France in Flanders during 1544; the commander had then described him as 'a very good man of war, and as meet to do his highness service as any other that is come at this time'.

When the signal to engage the French fleet was given, the *Mary Rose* edged forwards. But immediately she began to heel over. Sir George's uncle, Sir Gawen Carew, hailed him from another vessel to ask what was happening. '**I have a sort of knaves whom I cannot rule**', replied Sir George. These were his last words; for his ship heeled further and further, until water poured in, and in less than a minute she sank to the bottom. Only about thirty of the crew survived. Henry VIII watched the proceedings from Southsea Castle in amazement; so did Carew's wife, who fainted at the sight.

The battle which followed was inconclusive, but the upshot was the withdrawal of the French fleet.

What happened to the *Mary Rose*? Some French sources claimed that she was sunk by gunfire, but this seems altogether unlikely. Part of the trouble may have been that the ship had been rendered dangerously topheavy by the addition of large guns and extra men. The main cause, however, was surely negligence and mishandling. Sir George himself was possibly at fault; his conduct in the previous year's campaign (in which he was taken prisoner) was described as 'more forward than circumspect', betraying a rashness which is hardly appropriate to a ship's commander. But the near-contemporary account by his brother's biographer, like Sir George's own words, pins the blame on the crew:

> It chanced unto this gentleman, as the common proverb is – the more cooks the worse pottage: he had in his ship a hundred marines [i.e. sailors], the worst of them being able to be a master in the best ship within the realm; and these so maligned and disdained one the other, that refusing to

do that which they should do, were careless to do that which was most needful and necessary, and so contending in envy, perished in frowardness.

For over 400 years the *Mary Rose* lay on the muddy sea bed a mile off Portsmouth. Large-scale efforts to raise her in the summer of 1545 failed ignominiously. In the nineteenth century some cannon, timbers, and other objects were raised. Finally, a remarkable operation in the early 1980s recovered the surviving half of the ship's hull, together with numerous remains and artefacts which had been wonderfully preserved in silt, offering a unique time capsule from the Tudor age: guns, bows, arrows, tools, surgical instruments, personal items, shoes, skeletons, the stones of eight varieties of plums – and even the bones of rats which had no time to desert the sinking ship.

CAROLINE
of Ansbach
(1683–1737)

I have now got an asthma. Open the window. – Pray.
Lord Hervey of Ickworth, *Memoirs of the Reign of George II*
(edited by Romney Sedgwick, 1952)

Poor Caroline! – stifled at the last, and long before. The life of a queen of Great Britain and Ireland, wife to George II, proved to be no bed of roses. Somehow she managed to keep, to the very end, patience and a strong, dry sense of humour; and how much she needed them! She was expatriated in a country whose language she spoke badly, mingling English with her native German and with rough French. She was intellectually curious, fond of reading and art – while all around her were philistines; like his father, her husband detested all 'boets and bainters' except artists who portrayed fat nudes. She was spirited and sociable, and the dead hand of Hanoverian frigidity closed around her. When she made friends in one quarter, she automatically made bitter enemies in another. She might have run the country efficiently, had she had more opportunities; but small thanks she received. The family she joined and produced – oh, her family! When she married George, the electoral prince of Hanover, could she have any foresight of such a course of feuds, small-minded vindictiveness, and absurdity?

There was her father-in-law, George I, the first Hanoverian king of Britain; a man of extreme dullness, pettiness, and ignorance. When he came to the throne in 1714, he brought his son and daughter-in-law with him to a strange, uncivilized land. Towards Caroline he professed affection, as far as he was capable of that unmanly emotion; but between father and son there was a long-standing sullen hatred, which in 1717 flared into open hostility. The occasion was the christening of Caroline's second son; the causes are too complex and ludicrous to explain here; the result was that Caroline and her husband were expelled from St James's Palace, harassed, and threatened with disinheritance until a cool reconciliation took place in 1720.

Then there was her eldest son, Frederick Louis. Immediately after his birth in 1714, his parents seem to have taken a violent dislike to him – an antipathy that seems initially inexplicable except as a hereditary Hanoverian trait, although later events partly justified it. Frederick grew up to be a decent fellow – resentful, deceitful, shiftless, and immature. He allied himself to the parliamentary opposition; was banished from court; and took some revenge by writing *L'Histoire du Prince Titi*, a satire in the guise of a fairy tale, in which he lampooned his parents as 'King Guinea' and 'Queen Tripe'. When Caroline lay dying, Frederick was expressly forbidden to visit her. George then described him as a 'false, lying, cowardly, nauseous puppy', while the Queen went even further: **'At least'**, she said, **'I shall have one comfort in having my eyes eternally closed – I shall never see that monster again'**.

Her eldest daughter, Princess Anne, was also forbidden to

attend Caroline's deathbed. Anne had not always been in disfavour; her mother was very sympathetic when, in 1733, Anne married the dwarfish, hunchbacked, halitotic Prince of Orange – who, according to the Queen's confidant, Lord Hervey, 'looked behind as if he had no head, and before as if he had no neck and no legs'. Caroline's comment (in French, the usual language of her family) on the wedding-night was characteristic: 'When I saw that monster coming in to go to bed with my daughter, I thought I would faint'. But, a couple of years later, Anne disgraced herself by a fruitless attempt to return from Holland to England to deliver a child; this put the King to inconvenience and, worse, to expense – so she was never forgiven.

As for her husband – by and large they got on well together; she took his measure soon enough. But a cheerful, convivial, intelligent woman cannot have been wholly pleased by a stiff, vain, peevish, intolerant man. And, unlike him, she had no licence to pursue pleasures elsewhere. Although Caroline was a statuesque blonde, she was not large enough to satisfy the King, who followed his father's preference for women who 'rival the bulk and dignity of the ox' – the phrase comes from Lord Chesterfield, who also described two of George I's overt mistresses as 'considerable specimens of the King's bad taste and strong stomach'. George II made no secret of his liaisons (indeed, he exaggerated them to boost his vanity), on one occasion writing a letter begging Caroline to pimp for him in France: 'A pleasure which I am sure, my dear Caroline, you will be happy to procure for me, when I tell you how much I wish it'. However much Caroline was prepared for normal regal infidelity, such insolent stupidity must have been all but intolerable; but her repressed bitterness did not emerge until she lay on her deathbed and expressed her wish that the King should marry again. Sobbing convulsively, George gasped out the words 'No – I shall have mistresses'. '**Ah! my God!**' exclaimed Caroline – she frequently invoked God, and no wonder – '**That won't stop you**'.

Caroline's fatal illness became apparent on 9 November 1737. For years she had been suffering from an umbilical rupture, and out of embarrassment had kept quiet about it; but now she had unconcealable pains in the stomach and bowels, and vomited frequently. Physicians came, consulted, and prescribed various remedies – much the same kind of useless treatment that Charles II had been given (see p. 32). On 17 November she literally bust a gut, exuding all the contents of her stomach and bowels – an event which Alexander Pope, not showing such a Christian spirit as he displayed on his deathbed (see p. 142), celebrated in a savage epigram:

> Here lies wrapt up in forty thousand towels
> The only proof that Caroline had bowels.

Nor was the King's behaviour much comfort to her. Away from her bedchamber, he spent hours praising her as the finest woman who ever lived (and indirectly lauding his own goodness and heroism); but when he came to see her, he did little but reprimand her for not sleeping or eating and for having, as he tactlessly put it, 'eyes like those of a calf about to have its throat cut'. On the morning of 20 November she asked a physician how long she could survive; when he told her 'your majesty will soon find relief', she calmly answered **'So much the better'**. She died about ten o'clock in the evening of the same day, uttering the final words quoted above.

George II kept to his word, for once. He did not remarry; he had mistresses; he became increasingly unpopular; and he had the satisfaction of outliving his hated son. Frederick Louis died on 20 March 1751, of pleurisy – a result, according to his physicians, of his having been struck by a tennis ball three years earlier. If this diagnosis was correct, it was a sad fate for a keen sportsman who was president of the London Club which, in 1744, issued the earliest known version of the Laws of Cricket. His last words, spoken as he felt his distended stomach, were **'I feel death'**.

The circumstances of George's death on 25 October 1760 were described inimitably in a letter by Horace Walpole:

> He went to bed well last night, rose at six this morning as usual, looked, I suppose, if all his money was in his purse,

usual, looked, I suppose, if all his money was in his purse, and called for his chocolate. A little after seven, he went into the water-closet; the German *valet de chambre* heard a noise, listened, heard something like a groan, ran in, and found the hero of Oudenarde and Dettingen on the floor, with a gash on his right temple, by falling against the corner of a bureau. He tried to speak, could not, and expired.

Edith
CAVELL
(1865–1915)

Ask Mr Gahan to tell my loved ones that my soul I believe is safe, and that I am glad to die for my country.
Rowland Ryder, *Edith Cavell* (1975)

Edith Cavell, an East Anglian vicar's daughter, took up nursing in 1895 and went to Brussels twelve years later as matron of Belgium's first training school for nurses, the École Belge d'Infirmières Diplômées, where her life was uneventful until the Germans occupied Brussels in August 1914. Following the Battle of Mons in August-September 1914, Cavell sheltered two wounded British soldiers and helped them to reach neutral Holland. In subsequent months, in association with an underground group, she performed similar services for at least two hundred men – perhaps as many as a thousand – not only British and French soldiers, but also French and Belgian civilians.

On 5 August 1915 Cavell was arrested by the Germans, and tried on 7–8 October. The crux of the charges was not that she sheltered enemy troops, but that she was responsible for 'conducting soldiers to the enemy', an act which was a capital offence under Paragraph 58 of the German military code. On

11 October the death sentence was announced to her, and she was executed by a firing squad at dawn the next day.

The night before her death, Cavell was visited by an English clergyman, Stirling Gahan. It was to him she spoke the words which have become so famous, and so often quoted out of context, since their publication in *The Times* on 23 October 1915: **'This I would say, standing as I do in view of God and Eternity, I realize that patriotism is not enough. I must have no hatred or bitterness towards anyone'**.

Cavell's final private words, quoted above, were spoken to Paul le Seur, the German pastor who attended her at her execution. Probably the 'loved ones' to whom she referred were specifically her mother, her brother and two sisters, and her second cousin, Eddy, with whom she had had a frustrated romance in her youth.

Naturally, the killing of a woman, and a nurse, provoked enormous outrage. Cavell was seen as a martyr, a saint, an angel; she was enshrined as the embodiment of British womanhood, of dignity and courage (which indeed she showed), of beauty (which she neither possessed nor needed). Her death was strictly in accord with the prevailing law, but her offences seem to have been purely humanitarian acts. It appears unlikely that she ever stopped to consider her motives, or the consequences of what she was doing; hence her final statement that she was dying for her country is somewhat at odds with her expressed reservations about patriotism and her repeated injunction to Gahan to **'think of me only as a nurse who tried to do her duty'**.

King
CHARLES II
(1630–1685)

(a) **Let not poor Nelly starve**.
Gilbert Burnet, *History of My Own Time*, Vol. I (1724)

(b) **He had been**, he said, **a most unconscionable time dying; but he hoped that they would excuse it**.
Thomas Macaulay, *History of England* (1849)

(c) **Open the curtains that I may once more see day**.
Arthur Bryant, *King Charles II* (1955)

At least eight eye-witness reports of events at King Charles's deathbed are known, beside numerous second-hand contemporary accounts of varying reliability. The chief accounts are largely consistent, although there are some points of disagreement and some areas which remain vague.

The King's fatal illness began suddenly. On Sunday 1 February 1685 he went for a drive in a coach from the palace of Whitehall, supped heartily on his return, and spent some time in the evening with his chief mistress, the Duchess of Portsmouth (Louise de Kéroualle). When he got up on the following morning he was pale, confused, and almost unable to speak. He recovered somewhat, but later that morning, while being shaved, he had a severe attack of convulsions. A doctor standing by ventured to bleed him – although it was a capital offence to do so without permission of the King's chief ministers – and this treatment successfully restored the King to consciousness. For three more days the pattern continued – periods of apparent recovery alternating with convulsions – while a team of doctors tried out a variety of remedies: bleeding, purgatives, emetics, enemas, blistering, preparations to promote sneezing, and concoctions with such ingredients as paeony water, cowslip flowers, dried mallow root, melon seeds, and 'spirit of human skull'. They identified the illness as apoplexy, which was a reasonable diagnosis according to contemporary medical knowledge; but it now seems clear that Charles was suffering from a kidney complaint, and the doctors' ministrations may have served merely to hasten his end. There were several contemporary rumours that he had been poisoned, but such suspicions almost invariably accompanied a monarch's death, and in this case there is no reason at all to believe them.

By the evening of 5 February, Charles's condition was evidently grave. A priest having been secretly sent to him, he was converted to Roman Catholicism and received extreme unction. Then, surrounded by attendants and family, he began to make his farewells. He apologized for taking such a long time to die; but there is no evidence that he really used the phrase 'most unconscionable', which seems to be Macaulay's stylish addition to the King's wording. This wish to die quickly is ironically reminiscent of a deathbed statement by his father's inexorable opponent, Oliver Cromwell. On the night before his death, Cromwell refused a drink with the words '**It is not my design to drink or to sleep, but my design is to make what haste I can to be gone**'.

His wife, Queen Catherine, who had previously fainted in his presence, sent a message asking him to forgive her any offence she had ever caused him. '**Alas! poor woman!**' he replied, '**she beg my pardon! I beg hers with all my heart.**' He asked his brother, James, to look after the Duchess of Portsmouth; then he added his famous reference to Nell Gwynne – the illiterate, vivacious, indiscreet actress who had been his faithful and undemanding mistress since 1668 and had borne him two sons. (James, for all his faults and priggishness, did obey his brother's wishes: he paid all Nell Gwynne's debts and gave her a handsome income. But she did not long survive Charles, for she died in November 1687.) Next, Charles blessed the five of his natural sons who were present (his favourite son, the Duke of Monmouth, was in exile; see p. 109), and extended his benediction to all those in the room.

Before dawn on 6 February, Charles asked for the curtains in his room to be drawn back (see p. 61), then requested that an eight-day clock should be wound up. His life was running down irreparably: at seven o'clock he became breathless, at half-past eight he lost his speech. He was bled again, but now all treatment was useless, and he died shortly before midday.

Anton
CHEKHOV
(1860–1904)

It is some time since I drank champagne.
Ernest J. Simmons, *Chekhov* (1963), and Ronald Hingley, *A New Life of Anton Chekhov* (1976)

On 17 January 1904 the first performance of Chekhov's play *The Cherry Orchard* took place at the Moscow Art Theatre. It was perhaps the greatest triumph of his career; it was also a poignant occasion, for Chekhov was noticeably ill and was seized by a fit of uncontrollable coughing when he went on stage to receive the audience's acclamation. Following a lung haemorrhage, tuberculosis had been diagnosed in 1897, and Chekhov – who was himself a qualified physician – had moved away from Moscow, to live mainly in the Crimea, for the sake of his health.

In June 1904 the dramatist travelled with his wife – Olga Knipper, an actress at the Art Theatre – to the German spa of Badenweiler. There he died on the morning of 2 July. On the evening of his death he was improvising a comic story to amuse his wife; but he awoke in distress during the night and asked her to send for a doctor. '**Don't put ice on an empty heart**', he told her when she went to place a bag of cracked ice on his heart. On the arrival of a doctor, Chekhov said in German '**I am dying**'; and when the doctor ordered oxygen to be administered, Chekhov objected, saying '**Now nothing more is needed. Before they bring it, I'll be a corpse**'. In a final effort to stimulate his heart, the doctor prescribed champagne. Chekhov took a glass, turned to his wife with a smile, spoke the words quoted above, drank, lay down on his side, and died a few moments later. It was a sad, brave, laconic, haunting, thoroughly Chekhovian departure; the wine *motif* (see p. 10) makes a plaintive reappearance here.

Philip Dormer Stanhope, 4th Earl of CHESTERFIELD
(1694–1773)

Give Dayrolles a chair.
Matthew Maty, memoir of Chesterfield in Chesterfield's *Miscellaneous Works* (1777)

Philip Dormer Stanhope inherited the title Earl of Chesterfield in 1726, at which time he was already embarked on a successful public career that included appointments as British Ambassador at the Hague, Lord-Lieutenant of Ireland, and Secretary of State. His political accomplishments are now largely forgotten, with the possible exception of the contribution he made to bringing Britain into step with the modern world by introducing a bill to adopt the Gregorian calendar. Although his speech in the House of Lords on this occasion was greatly admired, Chesterfield admitted privately that he was utterly unable to understand the legal and astronomical niceties upon which the bill depended. Knowing that he could not inform his listeners, he determined to please them by his oratory.

This story is characteristic of Chesterfield and of the social and literary activities on which his posthumous fame rests. He is remembered, in the first place, for his somewhat negligent patronage of Samuel Johnson's *A Dictionary of the English Language*. Chesterfield initially encouraged the project, for he was anxious to have the standards of correct elegant English codified. But his concern with language was superficial, he had no patience with the long drudgery of scholarship, and he had little in common with Johnson. In the great nobleman's eyes the lexicographer must have seemed a contemptible figure, burdened with unprofitable learning, of uncouth appearance, provincial speech, and graceless manner. Chesterfield apparently ignored the work and its author for years until the time of its publication in 1755. Then he praised it highly; but it was too late. Johnson wrote him a gravely ironic letter, comparing a patron to 'one who looks with unconcern on a man struggling for life in the water, and, when he has reached ground, encumbers him with help'.

Of Chesterfield's own writings, the best-known are the frequent letters he addressed to his illegitimate son, Philip Stanhope. Intended to educate the young man in the ways of the world and to prepare him for a glittering political career (which in fact failed to materialize), they illustrate wonderfully an eighteenth-century notion of the model gentleman and of the path to social success.

'Manner', writes the solicitous but demanding father, 'is all in everything; it is by manner only that you can please, and consequently rise'. Knowledge, except of a practical kind, is futile; women are merely 'children of a larger growth'; feelings are an embarrassment, ideas a burden, morality an expedience; never mind the product, see the packaging. Johnson had a comment to make about these famous letters: 'They teach the morals of a whore, and the manners of a dancing master'. Of course this is unfair, but in the great lexicographer's eyes the nobleman must have seemed a disgusting figure, gilded with corrupt privilege, of cynical attitude, venal virtue, and insubstantial matter.

After his retirement from public life in 1755, Chesterfield's last years were clouded by gout, deafness, and failing eyesight. 'Lord Chesterfield', he once wrote sardonically, 'has been dead these twelve years, and has lost all the advantages of flesh and blood, without acquiring any of the singular privileges of a spirit'. He died – probably of dropsy – on the morning of 24 March 1773; but even on his deathbed he remembered his manners. When a visitor was announced, about half an hour before his death, in a faint voice he at once gave orders for a chair to be brought. The visitor, Solomon Dayrolles (died 1786), was a lifelong friend of Chesterfield and had served under him in Holland and Ireland. Matthew Maty (1718–1776), a physician, writer, and librarian who wrote a memoir recording the gracious Earl's last words, almost certainly derived the story from Dayrolles himself.

Frédéric
CHOPIN
(1810–1849)

Plus. [**No longer.**]
Casimir Wierzynski, *The Life and Death of Chopin* (1951), and Bernard Gavoty, *Frederic Chopin* (1977)

Chopin's last word (in French) was spoken in reply to a physician who asked him whether he was still suffering pain; it is attested by his friend Charles Gavard. Various other final utterances, both written and spoken, have been attributed to him, but all of them are disputed. The strength of mind which was mostly revealed in Chopin's music rather than in his life became apparent when he faced death.

Chopin, who left Poland in 1829 and came to Paris in 1831, struggled against lung disease for ten years. The concluding phase of his illness may perhaps be dated from the break-up of his eleven-year relationship with the writer George Sand (Madame Dudevant) in 1847. The following year, he fled from the revolution in France to Britain, where he was greatly admired; but the visit was not a success. Unlike Beethoven (see p. 8), Chopin, who spoke no English, did not form a favourable impression of British musical taste. He complained in a letter that 'every comment ends with the words: "Leik water", meaning that the music flows like water. I have never yet played to an Englishwoman without her saying: "Leik WATER!!" They all look at their hands and play wrong notes most soulfully. What a queer lot! God preserve them!'. The strenuousness of this tour further undermined his health, and his final public appearance took place at the Guildhall in London on 16 November 1848.

Returning to Paris, he became progressively weaker and died of consumption early in the morning of 17 October 1849. In accordance with his wishes, Mozart's Requiem (see p. 114) was sung at his funeral. He was buried in the Père-Lachaise cemetery, the resting-place of most of the eminent Frenchmen of the nineteenth century. As his coffin was lowered into the ground, earth was sprinkled onto it from a silver box containing Polish soil which had been given to him when he left his native country twenty years earlier.

Richard
CORBET
(1582–1635)

Good night, Lushington.
John Aubrey, *Brief Lives* (written *ca* 1670–80)

Not all seventeenth-century divines led lives of dull rectitude and selfless endeavour. The labours and sufferings of Peter Heylyn (see p. 78) seem an age removed – seem, oddly, to belong to an earlier, darker, age – from the worldliness and exuberance of Richard Corbet.

A nurseryman's son, Corbet (or Corbett, as he spelt his name) was educated at Westminster and Oxford before entering the Church. Having attracted the favour of the Duke of Buckingham and King Charles I, he was appointed one of the royal chaplains, then became Bishop of Oxford in 1628, and finally Bishop of Norwich in 1632. He was noted for his pulpit wit – though on one notorious occasion, when preaching before the King he was so distracted by a ring given him by the King that he kept losing track of his sermon and eventually had to abandon it.

It was not for any theological talents that Corbet was principally celebrated; nor even for his verses, collected in 1647, which show him to have been a lively minor poet. His reputation among his contemporaries centred on his conviviality, wit, and love of practical jokes. The clubbability and jocularity he showed as a young man, when he was a drinking-companion of Ben Jonson and other writers, did not vanish in his days of episcopal dignity. He was, to the last, 'very facetious and a good Fellowe' – so wrote John Aubrey, who had few higher terms of praise.

Corbet died in Norwich on 28 July 1635. A contemporary account states simply that he died 'like a Roman, bravely. As they prayed about him, he joined with them; prayers ended, he bid them all good night, and died'. According to Aubrey, however, his farewell was addressed specifically to Thomas Lushington. Lushington (1599–1671) was Corbet's chaplain, and a man of similar temper: witty, indiscreet, convivial. One of Aubrey's anecdotes uncorks the flavour of their friendship:

> His Chaplain, Dr Lushington, was a very learned and ingeniose man, and they loved one another. The Bishop sometimes would take the key of the wine-cellar, and he and his Chaplaine would goe and lock themselves in and be merry. Then first he layes downe his Episcopall hat – *There lyes the Doctor*. Then he putts off his gowne – *There lyes the Bishop*. Then 'twas, *Here's to thee, Corbet*, and *Here's to thee, Lushington*.

Thomas CRANMER
(1489–1556)

Then was an iron chain tied about Cranmer, whom when they perceived to be more steadfast than that he could be moved from his sentence, they commanded the fire to be set unto him. When the wood was kindled and the fire began to burn near him, stretching out his arm he put his right hand into the flame, which he held so immovable (saving that once with the same hand he wiped his face) that all men might see his hand burned before his body was touched.... His eyes were lifted up into heaven, and oftentimes he repeated his '**unworthy right hand**' so long as his voice would suffer him; and using often the words of Steven, '**Lord Jesus, receive my spirit**', in the greatness of the flame he gave up the ghost.

John Foxe, *Acts and Monuments* (5th edition, 1596–7), commonly known as 'Foxe's Book of Martyrs'

After the deaths of Ridley and Latimer (see p. 99), Cranmer was kept imprisoned in Oxford. The former bishops of London and Worcester were dispensable, whereas the former Archbishop of Canterbury was thought to hold the key to the success of Queen Mary's attempt to reintroduce Roman Catholicism into England. If Cranmer recanted, the Reformation would be discredited and the people might follow the path back to Rome.

Cranmer was not thought to be a strong and resolute man; rather, he was a studious theologian who had attained high office almost by accident. After studying at Cambridge, being ordained, and lecturing in divinity at the university, he had come to favour by aiding Henry VIII to annul his marriage to Catherine of Aragon – 'that man hath the sow by the right ear', Henry commented. Appointed Archbishop of Canterbury in March 1533, Cranmer supported the King's claim to supremacy of the Church but remained basically conservative in his attitudes. It was not until the reign of Edward VI that he undertook a thoroughgoing plan to turn England to Protestantism; then Cranmer himself compiled most of the Book of Common Prayer (1549, 1552) and drew up the Forty-Two Articles (later reduced to thirty-nine) which still serve as the basis of Anglican doctrine. He remained unconcerned with affairs of state, and was recognized as a charitable and generous man – also a relatively tolerant one, although he cannot be totally acquitted of responsibility for the burning of sundry heretics and eccentrics during his primacy.

Against his judgment, Cranmer was persuaded to support Edward's wish to be succeeded by Lady Jane Grey. After her failure to secure the crown, and Mary's accession, he was sent to the Tower of London and, in November 1553, convicted of treason. In March 1554 he was sent to Oxford with Ridley and Latimer; at his final trial eighteen months later he was convicted of heresy, and subsequently excommunicated and humiliatingly degraded. Now every effort was used to make him disavow Protestantism: flattery, entreaty, promises, threats. Under this barrage he yielded and signed a series of increasingly abject recantations, ultimately recognizing papal supremacy.

On the morning of 21 March 1556 Cranmer was led to St Mary's church, Oxford, where he was to declare publicly his revised opinions. After hearing a sermon bitterly attacking him – it may have been only at this point that he realized that he was going to be executed in any case – he began his speech with a number of basic moral exhortations, and went on to declare '**my very faith how I believe**'. Then, to the astonishment of most of the audience, boldly he denounced the Pope and his doctrine and recanted his own recantations '**as things written with my hand contrary to the truth which I thought in my heart**'. He continued: '**And forasmuch as my hand offended, writing contrary to my heart, my hand shall first be punished therefore; for may I come to the fire, it shall be first burned**' (an echo of Matthew 18:8: 'Wherefore if thy hand or thy foot offend thee, cut them off, and cast them from thee: it is better for thee to enter into life halt or maimed, rather than having two hands or two feet to be cast into everlasting fire'). He was hurriedly led away to the stake; and there he kept his promise.

CRAZY HORSE
(1841?–1877)

Father, it is no use to depend on me. I am going to die.
Stephen E. Ambrose, *Crazy Horse and Custer* (1976)

The name of Crazy Horse – which he took over from his father – may have inspired the popular image of him as a reckless warrior, the wildest of the hostile Sioux who fought against the white man's encroachment over the Great Plains area of North America. In truth, for most of his life he seems to have been a quiet, reserved man, a skilled but prudent warrior, and an able tactician, always realistic in his assessment of a conflict.

By his mid-twenties Crazy Horse was one of the acknowledged leaders of the Oglala tribe in Dakota. For a decade he was involved in scattered conflicts with the white man, culminating in the battle of Little Big Horn in June 1876. There the combined forces of Crazy Horse and Sitting Bull, the leader of the Hunkpapa tribe, annihilated a US battalion under the command of General G. A. Custer. This victory, however, proved futile. In the following year, with his people constantly harassed by the army and on the verge of starvation, Crazy Horse surrendered and was taken to the Indian agency based on Camp Robinson in Nebraska.

In the next few months he found no peace or satisfaction – only divisions and envy among the Sioux themselves, and mutual distrust and broken promises in his parleys with the white man. When his arrest was ordered, on the grounds that he was planning further hostilities, Crazy Horse fled. But two days later, on 6 September, he was persuaded to give himself up again and come to Camp Robinson to negotiate with the commanding officer. It was a trick; on his arrival he was immediately escorted to the guardhouse. Terrified and desperate, he struck out against his captors, drew a concealed knife, and forced his way out onto the parade ground. There, with his arms pinioned by his former ally Little Big Man, he was bayoneted by soldiers.

He died shortly afterwards, on a bed in the adjutant's office. The only people present were a formidable seven-foot-tall Miniconjou warrior called Touch-the-Clouds and Crazy Horse's father, now known as Worm.

René
DESCARTES
(1596–1650)

Ah! my dear Schluter, this is it; I must go now.
Adrien Baillet, *La Vie de Monsieur Des-Cartes* (1691)

Queen Christina of Sweden (1626–1689), one of the most learned women of her time, wished to surround herself with famous scholars and make her court one of the cultural centres of Europe. In 1647 she began a correspondence with the Frenchman René Descartes, who for a decade – since the publication of his *Discourse on Method* in 1637 – had been one of the most famous and controversial philosophers, the chief representative of a new rationalist philosophy on scientific principles which is now accepted as the foundation of modern metaphysics. But when the Queen invited him to Sweden, he made as many excuses as he decently could; he was extremely reluctant to leave dull, temperate Holland, where he had lived since 1629, and travel to a country which he envisaged as a 'land of bears, between rock and ice'.

Finally yielding to Christina's entreaties, Descartes arrived in Stockholm in October 1649. Although he was warmly welcomed, he soon found that not everything was to hisss liking. To start with, there were jealousies between the scholars attending the Queen. Next, the climate was abominable: 'men's thoughts freeze here in the winter months, just like the water', Descartes complained. In addition, the Queen insisted that her philosophy lessons should take place at five o'clock in the morning; to Descartes, who for most of his life had been accustomed to stay in bed until midmorning, this was an intolerable hardship. He had elevated indolence to an intellectual principle: 'The chief rule which I have always observed in my studies, and which I believe has helped me most to acquire whatever knowledge I have, has been never to spend more than a very few hours daily in thoughts which occupy the imagination, and a very few hours yearly in those which occupy the understanding, and to give all the rest of my time to the relaxation of the senses and the repose of the mind'.

Such an unwontedly rigorous regime quickly broke Descartes's health. On 1 February 1650 he caught a chill which soon developed into pneumonia. After taking to his bed, he was delirious for several days; but on the seventh day of his illness he recovered his senses and, according to his disciple Claude Clerselier, made the following statement: **'My soul, you have been a captive for a long time; now is the time when you must leave prison, and throw off the trammels of this body; this separation must be borne with joy and courage'**.

This speech is almost too good to be believed, for it encapsulates an idea central to Descartes's philosophy: the dualism of soul (or mind) and body. He believed that the body, and the whole material world, operated on purely mechanistic principles, according to God's established laws. Therefore animals are mere automata, like clocks, whereas man is distinguished by also possessing a rational soul, independent of the body and immortal – 'the ghost in the machine', as a modern philosopher has mockingly called it. This notion was really a corollary of Descartes's most famous proposition. As he describes in the *Discourse on Method*, he began his philosophical investigations by rejecting everything that he had learnt, all accepted wisdom, all the evidence of his senses, and even his own thoughts. But, even if thoughts were illusions, one thing remained which could not be denied: the act of thinking – and, consequently, the existence of a person performing this act. *Cogito ergo sum*: *I think, therefore I am*; and it seemed to follow that, if this 'I' existed as a substance whose whole nature consisted of thinking, then it was entirely separate from the body.

On 10 February Descartes ate some biscuits and for the first time expressed a hope that he could recover. In the evening, however, he fainted while sitting by the fire with Henry Schluter, a young German valet who had accompanied him

Descartes

to Sweden. When he regained his senses, Descartes spoke the almost untranslatably idiomatic French sentence ('**Ah! mon cher Schluter, c'est pour le coup qu'il faut partir**') of which a version is given above; he was then taken to bed, and was unable to speak again. He died peacefully at four o'clock the next morning.

Emily
DICKINSON
(1830–1886)

**Little Cousins,
Called back.
Emily**.
The Letters of Emily Dickinson, edited by T. H. Johnson (1958);
R. B. Sewall, *The Life of Emily Dickinson* (1976)

Emily Dickinson's last recorded message was sent to her younger cousins, Louise and Frances Norcross, early in May 1886. The poet was fatally ill with Bright's disease (inflammation of the kidneys); she lost consciousness on 13 May, and died two days later. Her elder brother noted in his diary for 15 May: 'The day was awful. She ceased to breathe that terrible breathing just before the whistles sounded for six'.

The last message was characteristically brief and cryptic. Dickinson's editors and biographers remark that it incorporates a reference to the novel *Called Back* by Hugh Conway, which she had mentioned in an earlier letter to the Norcrosses, but they do not seem able to explain whether the reference has any precise significance. The main point is, surely, that she is expressing a view of death as a summons back from mortality to eternity. Life on earth, she often implies, is merely a brief lodging; our true home is elsewhere.

Few writers have written as often, as perceptively, or as variedly about death as Emily Dickinson. In her own words, she 'sang off charnel steps'. The whole of her reclusive spinster life was spent within the confines of a small farming village in Massachusetts, but from this narrow base she contemplated the bedrock reality of human life with piercing insight, presenting the great dramas of existence in terms of concrete homely things:

> The only news I know
> Is bulletins all day
> From immortality.

Death appears in many guises in over 500 of her epigrammatic, teasing poems. Death is a terror, a hideous jest, a welcome relief, a passport to eternal happiness, a subtle seducer. It is a familiar domestic event: the stopping of a clock, closing of a door, drawing of a curtain, breaking of a cup. The very act of dying is portrayed several times, with attitudes ranging from cool detachment to remarkable empathy. The search for meaning continues even at the moment of death:

> I've seen a dying eye
> Run round and round a room
> In search of something as it seemed,
> Then cloudier become –
> And then – obscure with fog.

Perhaps the most extraordinary aspect of all is her tendency to imagine the moment of her own death (related to her tendency to see her every emotional loss as a kind of death), as in the poem 'I heard a fly buzz when I died'. Here the dying person, on the threshold of eternity, is still tied to the petty irritations and distractions of mortal life; at the expected moment of revelation a fly interposes itself 'with blue – uncertain stumbling buzz – / Between the light – and me'.

Only seven of Emily Dickinson's poems were published during her lifetime, and several of these were disimproved by editors' efforts to iron out her oddities. Like her near-contemporary Gerard Manley Hopkins (see page 83), she was too unconventional for her time. At a first glance, some of her verses can look like amateurish whimsy, but the seeming naivety is deceptive, concealing sophisticated artistry and brilliantly original insight.

Emily Dickinson's niece, Martha Dickinson Bianchi, refers to her aunt's 'briefest last message' ending with the words **'I must go in, the fog is rising'**. Unfortunately she fails to offer a source for this haunting phrase.

Denis DIDEROT
(1713–1784)

Whatever harm do you think that can do me?
André Billy, *Vie de Diderot* (1932), and Lester G. Crocker, *Diderot: The Embattled Philosopher* (1966)

On 31 July 1784 Denis Diderot dined at his home in Paris with his wife, his son-in-law, and a doctor who had called to see him. The philosopher was in poor health, having suffered two recent strokes, and had talked several times about the imminence of his death, but his appetite remained hearty.

He had always been rather a gourmand, perfectly capable of demolishing a whole meat pie or cheese; his letters contain numerous references to enormous meals followed by agonizing indigestion. More than just an incidental weakness, this was a symptom of his appetites in general, of his enormous vitality, of the careless profusion of his thought and writing. Nutrition was, even, a cardinal point in Diderot's materialistic philosophy of the origin of life: eating was the process by which inorganic material becomes organic, by which potential energy and latent sensitivity turn into actual energy and active sensitivity.

On this occasion, Diderot consumed soup, mutton, and chicory. He then took an apricot, whereupon his wife, Antoinette, remonstrated with him. Probably she was only thinking of his health, but after forty years of an unsuitable quarrelsome marriage the unreliable, flagrantly unfaithful husband automatically rejected any advice from the narrow-minded, scolding wife. '**Whatever harm do you think that can do me?**' he replied, and ate the fruit. Still unsatisfied, he started to reach for a bowl of stewed cherries. As he did so, a slight cough escaped him; when his wife asked him a question, he made no reply; he was dead.

An autopsy found that, among his other ailments, his gall bladder was completely dry and contained twenty-one stones.

By his abrupt death, Diderot at least escaped a scene which he dreaded: the inevitable attempt of a priest to reconcile him to the Church on his deathbed. By the age of thirty-five he had reached a position of agnosticism, viewing 'any meditation about the Beyond and death as useless, futile, and depressing'; later he became militantly atheistic, ascribing most of the crimes and corruptions of mankind to belief in a god, and violently opposed to all religions, to Christianity in particular. His opinions were notorious but, surprisingly, his son-in-law persuaded a priest to give Diderot a Christian (and splendid) burial. It was an inappropriate fate for the corpse of a man who, on the evening before his death, reputedly asserted to a visitor that 'the first step towards philosophy is doubt'.

Sir Everard
DIGBY
(1578–1606)

'Twas his ill fate to suffer in the Powder-plott. When his heart was pluct out by the Executioner (who, *secundum formam* [following custom], cryed, Here is the heart of a Traytor!) it is credibly reported, he replied, **'Thou liest!'**.
          John Aubrey, *Brief Lives* (written *ca* 1670–80)

Sir Everard Digby, born in Rutland, inherited a large estate on his father's death in 1592, and obtained a place in Queen Elizabeth's household. He was knighted soon after the accession of James I in 1603.

Coming under the influence of the Jesuit John Gerard, Digby was converted to Catholicism about 1599. In 1605 he was persuaded to join in the Gunpowder Plot, and given the responsibility of organizing an uprising in the Midlands. A few days after the failure of the plot he was captured in Staffordshire, and brought to trial in Westminster Hall on 27 January 1606 with seven other conspirators. Digby alone pleaded guilty, making a long speech of extenuation and repentance. Convicted of high treason and sentenced to be hanged, drawn (i.e. disembowelled), and quartered, he was executed in St Paul's churchyard three days later. On the scaffold he made another penitent speech, declaring that he would not have joined the conspiracy if he had fully appreciated its treasonable nature.

Aubrey, writing some seventy years after Digby's death, described him as 'a most gallant Gentleman and one of the handsomest men of his time'; but his account of Digby's last words perhaps relies on a credulous reception rather than a credible report.

Benjamin
DISRAELI
1st Earl of Beaconsfield
(1804–1881)

I had rather live, but I am not afraid to die.
W. F. Monypenny and G. E. Buckle,
The Life of Benjamin Disraeli (1929)

Benjamin Disraeli died on 19 April 1881 at his house in Curzon Street, London. Surmounting the handicaps of prejudice against his Jewish ancestry (born into the Jewish church, he had been baptized in 1817), vast debts, and a reputation for mere flashiness in dress and thought, he had risen in politics to become leader of the Conservative party, and Prime Minister of Great Britain in 1868 and from 1874 to 1880.

Several of Disraeli's deathbed sayings are recorded (most of them deriving from an account by Sir Philip Rose, his right-hand man). The one quoted above was probably his last, stoic utterance. Earlier he had said: '**I have suffered much. Had I been a Nihilist, I should have confessed all**' — a sardonic reference to the tortures used to extract confessions from the revolutionary Nihilists in contemporary Russia. His continuing wit displayed itself again as he corrected proofs of his last speech in the House of Lords (to which he had been elevated in 1876) for Hansard, the official parliamentary report: '**I will not go down to posterity talking bad grammar**', he commented.

His most famous stroke of deathbed wit arose out of the unusually close relationship with Queen Victoria which he had formed during his second premiership. Disraeli handled the monarch with tact and flattery, addressing her as if she were the ruler and he merely her adviser — unlike his rival William Gladstone who, Victoria reputedly complained, 'speaks to me as if I were a public meeting'. In a note to the Queen during his final illness, Disraeli described himself as 'prostrate though devoted'; she in turn sent him flowers and several letters expressing warm wishes for his recovery. But when it was suggested that the Queen might visit him, Disraeli demurred. A thought of Victoria's obsessive devotion to her husband Albert, dead for twenty years, crossed his mind. '**No**', he said, '**it is better not. She would only ask me to take a message to Albert**'.

Isadora DUNCAN
(1878–1927)

Adieu, mes amis. Je vais à la gloire.
[Goodbye, my friends. I am going to glory.]
Mary Desti, *Isadora Duncan's End* (1929)

In her expressive dancing, Isadora Duncan aspired to revive the simplicity and spontaneity of ancient Greece. Rejecting the restrictive formality of conventional ballet, she danced barefoot, in flowing robes, and was fêted throughout Europe as well as in her native America. On a visit to Russia in 1921 she became enthusiastic for communism, believing that the future of mankind lay in the solidarity of the working people, freed from commercialism and subservience. But, especially in the years of her decline, she displayed other, apparently contradictory tastes: for fast cars, first-class hotels, expensive food and drink, huge unpaid bills, wealthy lovers, and handsome young men.

In 1913 her two children, by different lovers, were drowned together in a car which ran into the River Seine. She herself was nearly killed in an accident in Russia in 1924, when the car in which she was travelling overturned into a ditch. But cars — the rectilinear machines so opposite to the swirling spirit of her dance — continued to fascinate her.

Soon after performing in Paris on 8 July 1927, Duncan moved to Nice. There she became infatuated with a young French mechanic who drove a Bugatti racing car; at the age of fifty, she seemed compelled to prove that she remained irresistibly attractive. She insisted that he was a Greek god in disguise, and pursued him blatantly until he agreed to take her for a drive on the evening of 14 September. As she stepped into the car she spoke the words quoted above — flamboyant, theatrical, euphemistic, in American-accented French — to her friend Mary Desti and a young Russian man. Sitting down, she threw round her throat a red painted crepe shawl, two yards long, which Desti had given her and of which she was particularly fond. The fringe of the shawl caught in the rear wheel of the car; when the vehicle moved forward, the shawl tightened, pulled her head down violently against the side of the car, and broke her neck.

John
ELWES
(1714–1789)

His appetite was gone — he had but a faint recollection of any thing about him; and his last coherent words were addressed to his son, Mr John Elwes, in hoping **'he had left him what he wished'**.

Edward Topham, *The Life of the Late John Elwes, Esquire* (1790)

John Elwes rode his mare only on grass, so that he would not be put to the expense of shoeing her. He refused to have his boots cleaned, lest the rubbing should wear them out. He collected old bones and crows' nests to burn on his meagre fire. He once dined on the remnants of a moorhen, brought out of the river by a rat. He was worth at least half a million pounds.

It is not surprising that he was the most notorious miser of his time. Yet the stock picture of the miser as a grasping, morose, humourless, friendless, narrow-minded old curmudgeon would certainly not offer a true and full portrait of the remarkable Elwes. He was a dandy and rake in his youth; he was a bad manager of his money, gambled heavily, speculated wildly, lent money without security, kept horses and a pack of foxhounds, was a connoisseur of food and drink (providing somebody else paid for them), and was known to his friends as a kind and witty man.

His peculiarity was, in the words of his biographer, 'the most gallant disregard of his own person, and all care about himself': he hated spending money on himself, and wanted everyone to believe that he was desperately poor. This trait of exorbitant self-denial ran in his family. After the death of his father, a wealthy brewer, his mother inherited £100,000 but reputedly starved herself to death. His uncle, Sir Harvey Elwes, practised economy to an extraordinary degree, living almost entirely on partridges and wearing his grandfather's clothes, but on his death in 1763 he bequeathed £250,000 to his nephew and heir.

In an uncharacteristic excursion into public life, Elwes sat as MP for Berkshire from 1774 to 1787, although he never spoke in the House of Commons. After his retirement from the House, his memory began to fail. He fell in love with a kitchen-maid, secreted money in hiding-places which he then forgot, and paced up and down at night crying 'I will keep my money, I will; nobody shall rob me of my property'. Only death, which came on 26 November 1789, could relieve him of his anxieties.

Elwes refused to educate his two natural sons (fathered on his housekeeper), on the grounds that 'putting things into people's heads is the sure way to take money out of their pockets'. Yet it was equally typical of his mixture of generosity and meanness that in his last words he expressed a wish that the fortune he was leaving his sons was sufficient for them.

Douglas
FAIRBANKS
(1883–1939)

I've never felt better.
Ralph Hancock and Letitia Fairbanks,
Douglas Fairbanks: The Fourth Musketeer (1953)

Douglas Elton Ulman, born in Denver, Colorado, showed fearless acrobatic talents even as a child, when he frequently terrified his mother by climbing on roofs and in trees and jumping from them. After their parents' divorce, he and his brother assumed their mother's surname by her first marriage, Fairbanks, and in 1900 Douglas went on the stage, where his vigour and athleticism gained him some renown.

After going into films in 1915, Fairbanks enjoyed more than a decade of enormous success as the swashbuckling hero of such straightforward but lively adventures as *The Three Musketeers*, *Robin Hood*, *The Mark of Zorro*, and *The Thief of Bagdad*. In these all-action silent films he performed nearly all his own stunts, became an expert user of swords and whips, and epitomized the smiling, clean-living, romantic, exuberant superman of popular fantasy. His marriage in 1920 to Mary Pickford, the blonde *ingénue* known as 'America's Sweetheart', even increased his popularity, once the public had got over the scandal of the stars' previous marriages. But Fairbanks and Pickford separated in the early 1930s; and, by then, changing public tastes, with the coming of the talkies, had virtually ended his career.

Fairbanks married again, lived in discontented obscurity for several years, and died on 12 December 1939 at his seaside home in Santa Monica, California. He had rarely known a day's illness, but on 11 December a sudden coronary thrombosis struck him. To his elder brother he commented: **'I'm not afraid of death, but I am afraid of being an** invalid, of being chained to a bed'. Shortly after midnight he awoke from a sedated sleep and called out to a male nurse: '**Please open the window and let me hear the sea**'. Having opened the window, the nurse asked Fairbanks how he was feeling. '**I've never felt better**', he replied, before falling into a sleep from which he did not awake.

In denying the imminence of death, Fairbanks followed one of the major traditions of dying speeches. In similar vein spoke Oliver Cromwell, on the morning of his death (3 September 1658): '**You physicians think I shall die. I tell you, I shall not die this hour; I am sure on't**'. Likewise, the American Mormon leader Brigham Young (1801–1877) died after saying, according to some accounts, '**I feel better**'. The best-known example is attributed to the British statesman Viscount Palmerston (1784–1865): '**Die, my dear doctor? That's the last thing I shall do**'. This is, however, apocryphal; Palmerston's real last words, reflecting his true bureaucratic character, were '**That's Article ninety-eight; now go on to the next**' (see Herbert C. F. Bell, *Lord Palmerston*, 1936).

Thomas
GAINSBOROUGH

(1727–1788)

We are all going to heaven, and Vandyke is of the party.
William T. Whitley, *Thomas Gainsborough* (1915), and
Jack Lindsay, *Thomas Gainsborough* (1981)

Thomas Gainsborough, one of the foremost English painters of portraits and landscapes, died of cancer at his London home (Schomberg House, in Pall Mall) on 2 August 1788. He had felt the first symptoms of his illness just seven months earlier, while a spectator at the famous trial in Westminster

Hall of Warren Hastings, former Governor-General of Bengal.

Gainsborough's final words reflect his vast admiration for the paintings of Sir Anthony van Dyck (or Vandyke), the Dutch artist who had worked in England from 1632 until his death in 1641. Gainsborough's own artistic career – his life was outwardly uneventful – divides itself neatly into three periods of almost equal length. After marrying and settling in his native county of Suffolk in 1746, he produced unpretentious portraits (such as 'Mr and Mrs Andrews'), and landscapes influenced by seventeenth-century Dutch masters. Moving to Bath in 1760, he became a fashionable painter and his portraits show increasing elegance; his work of this period (such as 'Blue Boy' and 'Mrs Portman') was particularly influenced by van Dyck. In his final phase, in London from 1774, his landscapes (such as 'The Watering Place') show the influence of van Dyck's teacher, Rubens.

Gainsborough's old friend William Jackson, a composer, recorded his optimistic last words, together with the artist's lament that he was dying just as he was beginning to accomplish something. While on his deathbed Gainsborough was reconciled with his great rival Sir Joshua Reynolds, with whom he had quarrelled many years earlier; Reynolds later spoke and wrote generously in praise of Gainsborough's work.

King
GEORGE V
(1865–1936)

(a) **How is the Empire?**

(b) **Bugger Bognor!**

After the death of King George V shortly before midnight on 20 January 1936, it was publicly given out (as in *The Times* of the following day) that his final words were '**How is the Empire**?'.

It seems undeniable that the King, addressing his private secretary, Wigram, did ask that question on the morning of his death, as he lay in bed at Sandringham. But they were certainly not his last words; for he followed them with the comment '**I feel very tired**', and, just after noon, while trying to sign an order paper in the presence of three statesmen, he apologized for keeping them waiting, explaining '**I am unable to concentrate**'.

There have been persistent rumours, however, that the King's last words were very different from those officially attributed to him. After a previous serious illness, he had convalesced in 1929 at the seaside resort of Bognor, in Sussex (it was this royal patronage that led to the addition of *Regis* to the town's name). So – the story runs – as the King was on his deathbed, the royal physician-in-ordinary, Bertrand Dawson (later Viscount Dawson of Penn), tried to reassure him by saying 'We'll soon have you back in Bognor, Sire'. The royal retort was pungent.

In a letter to *The Listener* in 1982, Leonard Miall stated that sources in Buckingham Palace had confirmed this account to Sir John Wheeler-Bennett, the official biographer of King George VI. Kenneth Rose, in his recent biography (*King George V*, 1983), is less convinced; while granting that 'The tale carries a certain plausibility', he is inclined to think that, if the King ever did utter those two notorious words, it was on an earlier occasion.

George V had succeeded to the throne on 6 May 1910 upon the death of his father, Edward VII, and it was to him that his father's uncontroversial last words were addressed. When his son told him that a horse of his had won a race at Kempton Park, the dying monarch replied '**Yes, I have heard of it. I am very glad**'.

Sidney GODOLPHIN
(1610–1643)

The civil war no sooner began . . . than he put himself into the first troops which were raised in the west for the King; and bore the uneasiness and fatigue of winter marches, with an exemplar courage and alacrity; until by too brave a pursuit of the enemy into an obscure village in Devonshire, he was shot with a musket; with which (without saying any word more, than, '**Oh God! I am hurt**') he fell dead from his horse; to the excessive grief of his friends, who were all that knew him; and the irreparable damage of the public.

Edward Hyde, Lord Clarendon,
The Life of Edward, Earl of Clarendon by Himself
(written 1668–70)

Sidney Godolphin, one of the paragons of his age, was born in Cornwall and educated at Exeter College, Oxford. During his short life he became MP for Helston, was employed on a diplomatic mission to Denmark, formed friendships with Lord Clarendon, Ben Jonson, Thomas Hobbes, Edmund Waller, and other notables, and proved himself an accomplished lyric poet. As a staunch Royalist, immediately upon the outbreak of civil war he joined the King's forces

Godolphin

and served under Sir Ralph Hopton. He was killed in a skirmish at Chagford in Devon on 9 February 1643.

Hobbes characterized him as one 'hating no man, nor hated of any'. Clarendon aptly contrasted his bravery in war and stoic death with the delicate and retiring nature he had shown in peacetime, when he was

> of so nice and tender a composition, that a little rain or wind would disorder him, and divert him from any short journey he had most willingly proposed to himself; insomuch as, when he rid abroad with those in whose company he most delighted, if the wind chanced to be in his face, he would (after a little pleasant murmuring) suddenly turn his horse, and go home.

The startling change in his habits was perhaps born of profound weariness and resignation – a temper of the times which is finely illustrated by the fate of Godolphin's peace-loving friend Lucius Carey, Viscount Falkland. According to the contemporary writer Bulstrode Whitelocke, Falkland insisted on participating in the Battle of Newbury (20 September 1643), although he was not a military man. To his friends he explained that he was 'weary of the times, and foresaw much misery in his own country, and did believe he should be out of it ere night'. Shot in the belly by a musket ball, Falkland tumbled from his horse and died at the age of thirty-four.

Johann Wolfgang von
GOETHE
(1749–1832)

Open the other shutter too, so that more light can come in!
K. W. Müller, *Goethes letzte literarische Thätigkeit* (1832);
reprinted in *Goethe: The Story of a Man*,
edited by Ludwig Lewisohn (1949)

The final words of Goethe are commonly quoted in the abbreviated form '**Mehr Licht!** [**More light!**], as if they were an appeal for spiritual illumination or, possibly, an exclamation on seeing a greater light at the end of mortal life. In the fuller version given by Müller they may appear merely as a prosaic instruction to his valet, uttered as the old poet lay dying in his bed in Weimar on 22 March 1832. A little while earlier, Goethe had made a similar comment: '**Let in more light. The darkness is disagreeable**'. The true interpretation probably lies between these extremes. There are many other instances of dying people making requests for windows or curtains to be opened. To cite but a few, there are Caroline of Ansbach (see p. 26); King Charles II (see p. 32); Douglas Fairbanks (see p. 55); and the English actor-manager Sir Herbert Beerbohm Tree, whose last words were '**Will you open the window?**'. Psychic needs, with a symbolic purport, may be partly responsible: the mind seeks final enlightenment; external reality, to which the mind desperately clings, has disappeared behind a closed curtain or window; or, on an even deeper level of myth, the window must be opened so that the soul or spirit, leaving the body at the instant of death, can fly away. But there are also evident physiological causes; the dying person will often experience breathlessness and a dimming of vision, and hence will desire air and light. The final moment of strangling darkness was imagined in this way in one of the greatest poems of Emily Dickinson (see p. 46):

> And then the windows failed – and then
> I could not see to see.

Other final words have been attributed to Goethe, such as a request to his daughter to give him her hand to hold. The adulators and would-be biographers clustering round his deathbed were unable to agree among themselves, and perhaps that discrepancy too has a symbolic application to such a many-sided, accomplished, but curiously elusive character. 'I do not know myself', Goethe once remarked, 'and God forbid that I should'.

There is a story, revelatory of the unforthcoming side of Goethe, of the meeting between him and the younger German poet Heinrich Heine in 1824. Heine had rehearsed speeches, epigrams, and compliments with which to impress and flatter his hero, but on encountering the great man he became completely tongue-tied. For his part, Goethe remained unhelpful, smiling benignly and inquiring patronizingly about Heine's health and experiences on his travels. Eventually poor Heine managed to stammer out that the plums he had eaten on his journey were the best he had ever tasted. It is no wonder that the humiliated young man's account of the experience reflects bitterly on Goethe's 'amiable condescension' and 'seventy-six years of calm and comfortable egoism', although it must be admitted that this encounter between Dionysus and Apollo perhaps belongs to a tradition of coloured anecdotes about disappointing meetings between great writers. When G. B. Shaw met August Strindberg, the conversation consisted mainly of embarrassed silences until Strindberg consulted his watch and announced 'At two o'clock I am going to be sick'. Of the meeting of James Joyce and Marcel Proust in 1921 various reports agree that the two novelists found no common ground: one version states that each man simply said that he had never read the other's work, and another that they spoke briefly about truffles. According to Thomas De Quincey, a man who had spent two days in a stagecoach with William Wordsworth and S. T. Coleridge could recall no gems from the poets' lips except for Wordsworth's exclamation at breakfast that the buttered toast looked as if it had been soaked in water.

Thomas
GOFFE
(1591–1629)

His Wife pretended to fall in Love with him, by hearing him preach: Upon which, said one Thomas Thimble (one of the Squire Bedell's in Oxford, and his Confident) to him: Do not marry her: if thou dost, she will break thy Heart. He was not obsequious to his Friend's sober Advice, but for her Sake altered his condition... 'Twas no long time before this Xantippe made Mr Thimble's Predictions good; and when he died, the last Words he spake were: '**Oracle, Oracle, Tom Thimble**', and so he gave up the Ghost.

John Aubrey, *Brief Lives* (written *ca* 1670–80)

Thomas Goffe (or Gough), the victim of this sorry misogynistic tale, was educated at Oxford, entered the Church, and became rector of East Clandon, Surrey, in 1620. There, despite the warnings of an old college friend, he married the widow of his predecessor. She, as shrewish as Socrates' wife Xantippe (or Xanthippe) was reputed to be, apparently made his life such a misery that he died soon afterwards. He was buried in East Clandon church on 27 July 1629.

Gough published a sermon and two Latin funeral orations, and also enjoyed some reputation as a dramatist: his three bombastic tragedies and a tragi-comedy were performed during his lifetime, although not published until later.

Nikolai
GOGOL
(1809–1852)

Give me! Give me! Come on, give me! – Quick, the ladder!
David Magarshack, *Gogol* (1957)

It is expected that priests and doctors, if unable to save the soul and life of a dying man, will at least comfort him. It was not thus in the case of the remarkable Russian writer Nikolai Gogol, who fell into the hands of a fanatic archpriest and six overzealous doctors. One hesitates to say that they caused or hastened his death – strictly, one must bring in a verdict of suicide through self-neglect while of unsound mind – but the combination of religious mania and unsuitable medication certainly did nothing to prevent or retard it.

Many bizarre events in Gogol's life show that he had long been suffering from hypochondria, various neuroses, and a series of psychosomatic illnesses. His obsession with dreams, madness, and persecution is noticeable in his masterpiece, the first part of *Dead Souls*, as well as in such stories as 'The Nose' and 'The Diary of a Madman' – works whose overall quality is that of a lucid, hilarious, but disturbing nightmare. Later, in the 1840s, while struggling to write the second part of *Dead Souls*, Gogol became increasingly possessed by a Messianic complex, believing that it was his duty to regenerate Russia through his writings. But how he could accomplish this grand mission was something he could never work out.

On returning to Russia in 1848 after twelve years spent mostly abroad, Gogol came under the influence of Father Matthew Konstantinovsky. This eloquent, half-educated, singleminded priest condemned the sinfulness of most worldly interests, including literature, and charged his followers to practise rigid asceticism. When Gogol showed him portions of the second part of *Dead Souls* on 4 February 1852, he condemned them as both profane and futile. Gogol, already in a weakened state, was terrified into submission; he gave up writing, fasted, and, a week later, burnt his manuscript. All will to live seemed to leave him. Refusing to eat or to listen to the well-meaning advice of his friends, he lay on a sofa in the house of his friend Count A. P. Tolstoy, waiting for death to release him from mental torment.

Six doctors were summoned on 20 February. They prodded Gogol, tortured him with questions, and finally agreed on a course of treatment which, even at that time, seemed a little odd. He was put into a tub of hot water, while ice-cold water was poured over his head. Then six leeches were applied to his nose – Gogol's famous long, sharp, sensitive, mobile, phallic nose, commemorated in the extraordinary noses featured in several of his works. No heed was taken of his cries of protest and terror. Mustard plasters were put on his hands and feet, ice on his head; he was forced to drink a concoction of marshmallow root and cherry-laurel water, and suppositories were administered. Delirious by now, Gogol kept calling **'Give me a drink! Give me the cask!'**. At eleven o'clock at night he cried out the words quoted above – perhaps merely wild feverish words, but perhaps a reminiscence of a sentence in his *Selected Passages from My Correspondence with Friends* which states that 'a ladder stands ready to be thrown down to us from heaven, and a hand is outstretched towards us, to help us mount in one bound'. He lost consciousness, and the medical treatment continued: a dose of calomel was administered, and hot loaves were placed round his body. According to some accounts he spoke again, incomprehensibly, soon after midnight: **'Go on! Rise up, charge, charge the mill!'**. At 8 a.m. on 21 February his sufferings ended.

Oliver
GOLDSMITH
(1730?–1774)

But Goldsmith could not sleep. His reason seemed cleared; what he said was always perfectly sensible; 'he was at times even cheerful'; but sleep had deserted him, his appetite was gone, and it became obvious, in the state of weakness to which he had been reduced, that want of sleep might in itself be fatal. It then occurred to Doctor Turton to put a very pregnant question to his patient. 'Your pulse', he said, 'is in greater disorder than it should be, from the degree of fever which you have. Is your mind at ease?' '**No, it is not**', was Goldsmith's melancholy answer. They are the last words we are to hear him utter in this world.

> John Forster, *The Life and Times of Oliver Goldsmith* (1855);
> Forster's source was an anecdote told by Samuel Johnson in 1777,
> reported in James Boswell's *The Life of Samuel Johnson* (1791)

'Toil, envy, want, the garret, and the jail': thus Samuel Johnson, one of Goldsmith's closest friends, characterized the perils of a scholar. Goldsmith cannot really be called a scholar, but the phrases – as Johnson knew – also encapsulate the life of a deserving writer without independent means in the eighteenth century, when the former system of support by wealthy patrons was giving way to dependence upon commercial publishers. Goldsmith escaped, at least, the last two stages. He managed to keep out of jail (apart from one youthful escapade), although arrest for debt threatened him on several occasions; and he had got away from living in dingy garrets in 1768 through the profits of his play *The Good Natured Man*, which enabled him to purchase decent chambers at 2 Brick Court in the Middle Temple. But toil, envy, and want – these were certainly his lot.

It would be easy, and somewhat misleading, to portray Goldsmith sentimentally or patronizingly as the unworldly, over-decent man exploited by unscrupulous publishers. On the other hand, it is surely unrealistic to claim – as Lord Macaulay did – that his distresses were wholly attributable to his own extravagance, addiction to gambling, and excessive generosity. The truth lies somewhere between, in the story of a man of unsophisticated manners, unattractive appearance, and erratic behaviour who arrived almost penniless in London in 1756 with no professional qualifications, drifted into literary hackwork, and found himself fettered to a treadmill.

He toiled, he drudged. There is not much sign of the glamour of authorship here. He wrote articles for reviews, magazines, and newspapers; essays; translations; prefaces; anthologies; biographies – of Beau Nash and Voltaire among others; histories of Greece, Rome, and England, primarily intended for schools; even a voluminous work on natural history. Somehow he also found time to write works which survive by virtue of their literary merit: the novel *The Vicar of Wakefield*, the play *She Stoops to Conquer*, the poems 'The Traveller' and 'The Deserted Village'. Yet, in a curious way, these seem almost incidental to his main labour of compilation. While it is almost entirely because of these greater works that Goldsmith is distinguished from dozens of other Grub Street writers scribbling to a publisher's commission, it is the miscellaneous works which are truly characteristic. Although pleasantly readable, they are marked more by fluency than by learning or insight. When Edward Gibbon facetiously told him that Alexander the Great fought against Montezuma, Goldsmith readily stitched the information into one of his patchwork histories. The news that Goldsmith was embarking on a *History of the Earth and Animated Nature* led Samuel Johnson to deliver a grave opinion: 'Goldsmith, Sir, will give us a very fine book upon the subject; but if he can distinguish a cow from a horse, that, I believe, may be the extent of his knowledge of natural history'.

The books were successful and profitable – but far more to the publisher than the author. In 1774, after fifteen years of full-time authorship, Goldsmith was as far as ever from escaping his drudgery. His debts were mounting to a figure

– over £2000, according to one contemporary estimate – which it seemed impossible to clear by writing. Envy being his one real moral failing, he was distressed by the worldly success of less talented but more plausible men. Overwork had made him ill; and the prospect of yet more work of the same kind was inescapable and intolerable. 'Such was the end', commented his biographer Forster, 'such the unwearying and sordid toil, to which even his six years' term of established fame has brought him! The cycle of his life was complete; and in the same miserable labour wherein it had begun, it was to close'.

The illness which came upon Goldsmith towards the end of March 1774 and culminated in death on 4 April was probably Bright's disease, inflammation of the kidneys. Overwork and anxiety undoubtedly aggravated his condition. So, perhaps, did his insistence on dosing himself with an unsuitable patent medicine. This may evoke an ironic comment on Goldsmith's pretensions to medical knowledge – for, although he was commonly titled 'Dr Goldsmith', his studies of medicine had been irregular and there is no record that he ever obtained a medical degree. But there is a further twist to the tale: the proprietors of this medicine were none other than the publishers (John Newbery, succeeded by his son Francis) for whom most of Goldsmith's work had been produced. Doubly, then, poor Goldsmith might be accounted one of the martyrs of the book.

Roosevelt
GREEN
(1956–1985)

What you people are about to witness is a grave injustice. I am about to die for a murder I did not commit, that someone else committed. I have nothing against anyone and I have no enemies. I love the Lord and hope that God takes me into his kingdom, and goodbye, mother.

Daily Telegraph, 10 January 1985

By a decision of the Supreme Court in 1976, the states of the United States were permitted to restore capital punishment if they wished. Initially, few executions resulted, but as more states took up the option and inmates of Death Row exhausted their appeal rights, the number increased markedly: five in 1983, twenty-one in 1984, a projected figure of sixty in 1985.

Roosevelt Green and an accomplice were convicted and sentenced to death in 1976 for rape and murder. The victim was an eighteen-year-old undergraduate who was abducted from a grocery store where she was working, raped, and shot twice with a high-powered rifle. Green's lawyers appealed on the grounds that he was not present when the murder was committed, and that the state of Georgia was administering the death penalty in an arbitrary and discriminatory way. The appeals were unsuccessful, and Green was executed in the electric chair on 9 January 1985. His mother was among the witnesses to whom he made a final statement proclaiming his innocence, just before the electrodes were attached to his body.

An execution in South Carolina two days later clearly revealed contradictory public attitudes. Opponents of capital punishment, protesting against a 'deepening bloodbath', staged a candlelight vigil outside the prison where the execution took place. Meanwhile, local businessmen handed out bumper stickers showing an electric chair with the slogan 'Use it', and one individual paraded with a placard reading: 'The electric chair is too good for scum'.

Sir Richard
GRENVILLE
(1541–1591)

Here die I, Richard Grenville, with a joyful and quiet mind, for that I have ended my life as a true soldier ought to do, that hath fought for his country, queen, religion, and honour, whereby my soul most joyful departeth out of this body, and shall always leave behind it an everlasting fame of a valiant and true soldier, who hath done his duty, as he was bound to do. But the others of my company have done as traitors and dogs, for which they shall be reproached all their lives, and leave a shameful name for ever.

Jan Huyghen van Linschoten,
Itinerario, voyage ofte schipvaert (1595–96)

The berserk spirit of old warriors seemed to live again in Sir Richard Grenville. His claim to be a direct descendant of the famous ninth-century Norman leader Rollo cannot be accepted literally, but it certainly had a metaphorical truth. A proud, ambitious, headstrong man, Grenville loved the challenge of fighting against overwhelming odds. Long before his famous final conflict he was renowned for the reckless courage he had shown in battle at Lepanto, in Hungary and Ireland, and as a privateer. The unfortunate men under his command were almost as much at risk as the enemy, such was his disregard of caution. For a party trick he used to eat wineglasses, remaining totally unmoved while blood poured out of his mouth.

In 1591 Grenville was appointed vice-admiral of the squadron of twenty-odd ships sent, under Lord Thomas Howard, to intercept the treasure ships expected to come from the West Indies to Spain. While waiting in the Azores, and suffering from an epidemic fever, on 9 September this fleet was surprised by the arrival of a flotilla from Spain numbering at least thirty ships, perhaps as many as sixty. Howard sailed away hurriedly, followed by all the other ships except Grenville's *Revenge* – a smallish vessel of 500 tons and with a complement of 250 men, which had been Sir Francis Drake's ship at the time of the Spanish Armada.

Grenville remained until the Spanish fleet was almost on top of him. He may have been delayed by embarking sick men, but more likely reasons lay in his own character: stubbornness, pride, overwhelming confidence, and inability to resist the prospect of a good fight. Eventually he tried to run his ship through the Spanish line, but the *Revenge* was becalmed and surrounded. She seemed helpless, but now Grenville was roused. Boatload after boatload of Spanish soldiers tried and failed to board the *Revenge*. Ship after ship attacked her and was beaten back – four were sunk and several others seriously damaged. Grenville himself was wounded three times, but for almost fifteen hours he maintained the fight. When his position had finally become impossible, he still refused to surrender; instead, he gave orders to his master-gunner to blow up the ship with all hands on board. The crew, being ordinary mortals, did not approve of this plan, and, without their commander's knowledge, negotiated a surrender on condition that their life and liberty were guaranteed.

Grenville, doubtless fuming, was taken on board the Spanish flagship, the *San Paulo*. There he died of his wounds a few days later, and was buried at sea (thus sharing a watery grave with his father, who was one of the victims of the *Mary Rose* disaster; see p. 25). As soon as his body sank, an immense storm arose. The *Revenge*, under tow, was smashed on rocks and sunk; dozens of Spanish ships foundered. The real cause of this cataclysm was probably an earthquake, but to superstitious sailors it must have seemed as if their superhuman enemy was still on the rampage.

Jan Huyghen van Linschoten, a Dutchman who was present in the Azores at the time, wrote a detailed account which includes Grenville's alleged last speech (supposedly spoken in Spanish). The authenticity of this speech has been disputed, and it is hard to accept it as a straight transcript of Grenville's actual words. It may, however, fairly reflect the gist of some utterance he made. When an English translation of Linschoten's work was published in 1598, the last sentence of this speech was omitted; in fact it was not printed in any English account before the nineteenth century. It is uncertain whether Grenville's bitter reproach was aimed at Howard or at his own crew, but in either case it was evidently too outspoken to be printed while many of the people involved were still alive and while it was expedient to promote the legend of Grenville as a true chivalrous hero.

HADRIAN
(76–138)

(a) **Wandering pleasant little soul,**
Guest and comrade of the body,
To what places are you going —
Frightful, savage, desolate —
Where you won't make your usual jokes?
Aelius Spartianus (?), 'De Vita Hadriani', in *Historia Augusta* (written *ca* 400?)

(b) **Many physicians have slain a king.**
Cassius Dio, *History of Rome* (written *ca* 220)

Composing verses at the point of death may be considered a rare activity. Prose is good enough for the final words of most people, although perhaps a Roman emperor, on the verge of deification, may transcend the normal course of events. Nor would such an oddity be out of keeping with the capricious and puzzling character of Hadrian, who died on 10 July 138 at Baiae (now Baia), on the Bay of Naples, after a long painful illness. He showed himself, according to Edward Gibbon, 'by turns an excellent prince, a ridiculous sophist, and a jealous tyrant'. He was a man of some culture, a great admirer of Greek civilization; an indefatigable traveller through all parts of the Roman empire – his visit to Britain in 122 resulted in the building of 'Hadrian's Wall', a rampart stretching from the Tyne to the Solway to defend the northern frontier of the Roman province; a scrupulous reformer of Roman law, finances, and morality; yet frequently displaying mean, superstitious, pederastic, vain, or cruel traits.

We cannot be certain whether Hadrian wrote this poem on his deathbed, if at all. The attribution rests solely on the *Historia Augusta*, a collection of brief biographies of the Roman emperors from 117 to 284, which states: 'It is said that he wrote these verses as he was actually dying'. But this is a suspect document. Although it was ostensibly composed by six authors about the end of the third century, many scholars now believe that it was written – for obscure reasons – by a single pseudonymous author at the end of the fourth century. In many places it is demonstrably inaccurate, sometimes wholly fictitious – although the account of Hadrian does seem to be largely authentic. However, a different story appears in the extant eleventh-century summary of the lost work of the Greek historian Cassius Dio (*ca* 150–235). This relates how Hadrian, longing for release from his illness, failed to persuade or compel anyone to kill him but hastened his death by indulging in an unsuitable diet, and died shouting a version of the popular joke about a man being killed by his physicians.

Nevertheless, the poem is comparable to the few other verses ascribed to Hadrian, and may be plausibly accepted as his. This strange – part jocular, part fearful – little address to his soul as it begins its journey into a dark afterlife has inspired many translations into English, among them two of particular interest. Alexander Pope (see p. 142) produced this version:

> Ah fleeting Spirit! wand'ring Fire,
> That long hast warm'd my tender Breast,
> Must thou no more this Frame inspire?
> No more a pleasing, chearful Guest?
> Whither, ah whither art thou flying!
> To what dark, undiscover'd Shore?
> Thou seem'st all trembling, shiv'ring, dying,
> And Wit and Humour are no more!

Lord Byron (whose own last words were '**I want to sleep now**') translated it thus:

> Ah! gentle, fleeting, wav'ring sprite,
> Friend and associate of this clay!
> To what unknown region borne,
> Wilt thou now wing thy distant flight?
> No more with wonted humour gay,
> But pallid, cheerless, and forlorn.

Neither translation captures the succinct directness of the Latin original and the odd effect of its cluster of diminutive forms in the first and fourth lines (*Animula vagula blandula... pallidula rigida nudula*).

Nathan HALE
(1755–1776)

I only regret that I have but one life to lose for my country.
from the memoirs of William Hull,
quoted by Henry Phelps Johnston, *Nathan Hale* (1914)

The American hero Nathan Hale graduated from Yale University and worked as a schoolteacher until the outbreak of the War of American Independence in 1775. He was then commissioned a lieutenant in the Connecticut militia, and promoted to captain at the beginning of the following year.

In September 1776 he volunteered for a reconnaissance mission behind the British lines. Disguised as a Dutch schoolmaster, he succeeded in obtaining information about the disposition of enemy troops, but on his way back he was captured and condemned to death for spying. He was hanged the next morning (22 September), after reportedly making a brief speech on the gallows.

The famous version of Hale's words presented above – it is often quoted with 'give' instead of 'lose' – comes from the memoirs of his friend Captain William Hull, who stated that he obtained details from a British officer who witnessed Hale's execution. But these memoirs were written decades after Hale's death; Hull himself had written an earlier account in which his dying words, although similar to the later version, appear in indirect speech and in a less polished form. Moreover, an anonymous newspaper report in 1782 gave another version of Hale's final speech: '**I am so satisfied with the cause in which I have engaged, that my only regret is, that I have not more lives than one to offer in its service**'.

Hull's revised version – which has served to inculcate patriotic sentiments into many generations of young Americans – may genuinely reflect the gist of Hale's final words, but it is hard to accept it as a verbatim record. Apart from the discrepancies between the various accounts, the well-known form of the words is suspiciously similar to a sentence in Joseph Addison's play *Cato* (1713):

> What pity is it
> That we can die but once to serve our country!

Heinrich
HEINE
(1797–1856)

Write! Write! Write! Paper! Pencil!
Louis Untermeyer, *Heinrich Heine* (1938), and
E. M. Butler, *Heinrich Heine* (1956)

Early in the morning of 17 February 1856, as he lay on his deathbed in an apartment near the Champs Elysées in Paris, Heine gasped out these words. A nurse, the only other person in the room, tried to put a pencil into his hand, but he was too weak to hold it, and he died almost immediately afterwards. It is idle to speculate about what Heine wanted to write; the point of the episode lies in the very compulsion to write. After a lifetime of literary activity, Heine was still in the state he described as 'a tomb without quiet, a death without the privileges of the dead. Dead men do not have to spend money, write letters, or make books'.

For eight years before his death Heine had been bedridden and agonized, suffering from partial paralysis, spinal pains, and deteriorating eyesight. Although the issue is still disputed, most authorities accept that the cause of his suffering was syphilis, and that he had contracted the disease from prostitutes after being jilted by his cousin Amalie just before his twenty-third birthday. Heine probably did not realize the situation, for his illness was never diagnosed, but the frequent association of love and death in his poetry surely springs from deeper sources than *Weltschmerz* or cynicism. By the age of thirty-five he was experiencing tormenting headaches and some degree of paralysis, and his decline over the years was inexorable. By 1848 he was helpless: 'My mind is so hungry for life, and my body is so crippled. I feel myself rotting; I see no one, talk to no one. It is as though I were buried alive.'

In this state, he changed his religious views. Having been born a Jew, reluctantly converted to Protestantism as a matter of expediency, and become a definite atheist, in 1851 he returned to belief in a personal God: 'Lying on one's deathbed', he wrote, 'one becomes sensitive and sentimental, anxious to be at peace with God and the world.... I have made my peace with God's creatures and their Creator.' The God he acknowledged, however, was not necessarily a just and lovable God; Heine not only besought him and prayed to him, but argued with him and reviled him for permitting the inequity of human existence. On the evening before his death Heine made his celebrated reply to an enquiry whether he had made his peace with God: **'God will pardon me – that's his profession'** (see p. 171 for Thoreau's reply to the same question). His long illness had given him the opportunity to become as prepared for death as anyone can be. 'Death, between you and me', he remarked, 'is the least thing to fear. It is dying which is terrible, not death – if there is such a thing as death. Death may be the final superstition.'

Heine had married an illiterate French shop-assistant, a sensual, slovenly, and shrewish woman. Although the marriage had not been very happy, she had never deserted him during his illness. But on the morning of his funeral, 20 February 1856, she went away secretly and did not return for a month. Heine's friend Karl Marx wrote about the incident to Friedrich Engels, his collaborator on the *Communist Manifesto*, offering an explanation that was characteristically cynical but shrewd about human nature: the ungrieving widow had gone off with a lover.

Peter
HEYLYN
(1600–1662)

He found himself taken with a violent Fever, occasioned (as was conceived by his Physician) by eating of a little Tansey at Supper. It seized him, May 1. 1662. and deprived him of his understanding for seven days: the eighth day he died; but for some hours before had the use of his Faculties restored to him, telling one of the Vergers of the Church, who came to him; '**I know it is Church-time with you, and this is Ascension-day, I am ascending to the Church triumphant, I go to my God and Saviour, into Joys Celestial, and to Hallelujahs Eternal**'.

George Vernon,
The Life of the Learned and Reverend Dr Peter Heylyn (1692)

The busy vicissitudinous life of Peter Heylyn, divine and author, mirrors the disputes and upheavals of mid-seventeenth-century England. Educated at Oxford, he was ordained in 1624 and, as a protégé of William Laud (later Archbishop of Canterbury), appointed chaplain to King Charles I in 1630. He distinguished himself by the fluency of his pen, publishing over fifty works – mainly concerned with theological controversies, although he also produced such miscellaneous works as *Microcosmus* (a geographical textbook) and *A Survey of France* (a lively memorial of his travels in France in 1625). A vigorous adherent of the High Church and Royalist party, he engaged in ceaseless, and often bitter and personal, debate with Puritans, Presbyterians, and other religious sectarians.

During the Civil War Heylyn was forced by the Parliamentary army to move from his home in Alresford, Hampshire; he joined the King at Oxford in 1642, where he was employed as the first editor of the Royalist propaganda newsbook *Mercurius Aulicus*. Having had his house plundered during the war, he seems to have led an impoverished and unsettled existence for several years before establishing himself at Abingdon in 1653. Despite misfortunes, even the loss of his eyesight around 1654, he continued to pour forth books and pamphlets, and upon the restoration of the monarchy in 1660 he was rewarded with appointment as sub-dean of Westminster.

Heylyn died on 8 May 1662. His reverential biographer, George Vernon (who was rector of Bourton-on-the-Water in Gloucestershire), records a strange premonitory dream that Heylyn had just before his fatal illness:

> That being in an extraordinary pleasant Place, and admiring the beauty and glory of it, he saw King Charles I. his Martyr'd Master, and heard him speaking to him in these words, viz. Peter, I will have you buried under your Seat at Church, for you are rarely seen but there, or in your Study.

Heinrich HIMMLER
(1900–1945)

He doesn't know who I am.
Roger Manvell and Heinrich Fraenkel,
Heinrich Himmler (1965)

The extravagant power of the head of the Gestapo and Commander-in-Chief of the German Home Forces waned in the spring of 1945. In April, when the collapse of Germany seemed imminent, on his own initiative he attempted to negotiate a surrender to Britain and the United States. Not only was the offer rejected, but Hitler ordered Himmler's arrest when he heard of it. Still protected by his entourage, Himmler escaped to Flensburg, near the Danish border, but the unconditional surrender of Germany to the Allies on

7 May 1945 left him with nothing to save but his skin. He shaved off his moustache, assumed an eyepatch and false papers, and fled with a few followers.

On 23 May British forces arrested a suspicious person near Lüneburg. Himmler's rudimentary disguise did not prevent his speedy identification, and in the evening he was taken to an interrogation centre in Lüneburg. Following the suicide of a high-ranking Nazi a few days before, the British knew of the phials of poison carried by their defeated enemies, and planned to search Himmler thoroughly but cautiously. A sergeant-major therefore ordered him to get undressed. Himmler, who seemed to be enjoying a resurgence of self-importance, stared at the soldier arrogantly and remarked to an interpreter '**He doesn't know who I am**'. 'Yes I do', replied the soldier, 'You're Himmler. Nevertheless, that's your bed. Get undressed.'

Himmler was stripsearched by the soldier and an army doctor. Finally, trying not to arouse his suspicions, the doctor looked into Himmler's mouth and noticed a small black capsule protruding from a gap in the teeth. Gently he put two fingers into the mouth; at that moment Himmler bit hard and wrenched himself away. His captors immediately turned him on his stomach and held his throat in an effort to stop him swallowing, administered emetics, and used a stomach-pump, but they were unable to prevent him from anticipating the course of justice. In fifteen minutes Himmler was dead of cyanide poisoning.

Thomas
HOBBES
(1588–1679)

(a) **I am about to take my last voyage, a great leap in the dark.**
traditional

(b) Confirmed also that Thomas Hobs died at Hardwick within 12 miles of Chatsworth, that on his death bed he should say that he was 91 yeares finding out a hole to go out of this world, and at length found it.
Anthony Wood, 'Journal', 10 December 1679 (printed in *The Life and Times of Anthony Wood*, edited by Andrew Clark, Vol. II, 1892)

The philosopher Thomas Hobbes died of a paralytic stroke on 4 December 1679 at Hardwick Hall, Derbyshire, the home of his patron the Earl of Devonshire. His life had been long – his birth was reputedly hastened by his mother's fright at the approach of the Spanish Armada – and his old age remarkably active. At eighty-four he wrote his autobiography in Latin verse; a year later he began a verse translation of Homer's *Iliad* and *Odyssey*, completed in 1675; and he continued writing on scientific subjects until his death.

Hobbes's alleged dying reference to a 'leap in the dark' has been frequently and variously quoted: in the form given above, as 'I am taking a fearful leap in the dark', and so on. Unfortunately it seems impossible to authenticate it. The earliest allusion that can be found to this phrase is a rather puzzling one in Sir John Vanbrugh's play *The Provoked Wife* (produced in 1697), where the character Heartfree remarks: 'So, now I am in for Hobbes's voyage, a great leap in the dark'. Heartfree, however, is referring to marriage rather than to death. One may deduce that there was a common story that Hobbes had described marriage, or death, or both, as a leap in the dark; but the phrase seems neither to occur in any of Hobbes's works, nor to be attributed to him by any reliable biographer. Later writers who have ascribed the phrase to him may simply be embroidering Vanbrugh's hint. For instance, John Watkins's *Characteristic Anecdotes of Men of Learning and Genius* (1808) states that Hobbes 'was very much afraid of death which he called "taking a leap in the dark" ', but Watkins offers no source for the phrase and does not claim that it was Hobbes's last utterance. Possibly it is one of those anonymous semi-proverbial sayings to which the name of a famous person has been attached – that of Hobbes, in this instance, because of his notorious agnosticism. Several other versions, apparently independent of Hobbes and Vanbrugh, are known. Thomas Brown (1663–1704), in his *Letters from the Dead*, refers to death as 'a leap into the dark'. Daniel Defoe, in *Moll Flanders* (1722), has 'make matrimony, like death, a leap in the dark'. Finally, the phrase bears a suspicious resemblance to one of the apocryphal last sayings attributed to Rabelais (see p. 144), which in Peter Le Motteux's preface to the Urquhart-Motteux translation of Rabelais (1693–1708) is rendered as 'I am going to leap into the dark'.

The contemporary account of Hobbes's death by Anthony Wood, the Oxford antiquarian, rests on hearsay and may be coloured by prejudice. Hobbes's theories of politics, theology, and mathematics embroiled him in continual controversies, and the choleric Wood had scant respect for him: he described him as an 'enimy to Universities, school-divinity, Aristotle, presbyterians, metaphysics', reported that he was 'an ill-natur'd man they say, proud, scornfull', and complained that Hobbes's masterpiece *Leviathan* 'hath corrupted the gentry of the nation, hath infused ill principles into them, atheisme'.

Another contemporary writer gives an account of Hobbes's death which contradicts both the other versions. Although (ironically) John Aubrey wrote his sketch of Hobbes for Wood's sake, as part of his generous offer to furnish biographical information for Wood's *Athenae Oxonienses*, he was a man of very different character – a Cavalier to Wood's Roundhead – and had known Hobbes personally for almost forty years. Aubrey, in the manuscript now commonly known as *Brief Lives*, describes Hobbes's end thus:

> Seven or eight days after, his whole right side was taken with the dead palsy, and at the same time he was made speechlesse. He lived after this seven days, taking very little nourishment, slept well, and by intervals endeavoured to speake, but could not.

Gerard Manley HOPKINS
(1844–1889)

I am so happy, so happy.
Eleanor Ruggles, *Gerard Manley Hopkins* (1947)

The Revd Gerard Hopkins, S J, died of typhoid in Dublin on 8 June 1889. His death caused no ripples outside his immediate circles. As Professor of Classics at University College, Dublin, he was a conscientious teacher but an undistinguished scholar. Very few people knew that he was a poet; apart from one excerpt, none of his verse had been published during his lifetime. His superiors in the Jesuit order were aware of his poetical inclinations, and prepared to tolerate them to some degree, but they rejected the poems he submitted for publication in Jesuit periodicals. A few correspondents were familiar with his literary activities – principally Robert Bridges (later Poet Laureate), a writer of classical tastes who published the first selection of Hopkins' verse in 1918. Bridges was capable of discerning a touch of original genius in the poems which Hopkins sent him. But he also saw much that seemed wilfully odd, obscure, even incompetent. He sympathized, sighed, continued writing his own relatively conventional poems, and waited for almost thirty years before daring to unleash his idiosyncratic friend on the public.

Why, then, was Hopkins so happy at his death? Probably because he saw it as the supreme sacrifice. One of the most brilliant Oxford undergraduates of his time, and talented in art as well as literature, he had renounced all worldly ambitions to join the Jesuits and spend years in severe training, pastoral work in the slums of Liverpool and other industrial cities, schoolmastering, and an unsatisfying exile in Dublin. From the age of twenty-one he had embarked on an annihilation of himself – poverty, chastity, obedience, mortification, and the eradication of unruly individual desires. Now the process was complete; death was the ultimate self-denial, and he had nothing more to fear; his parents had come to see him, he had received extreme unction, the body was totally subdued at last, and the soul was free:

> Flesh fade, and mortal trash
> Fall to the residuary worm; world's wildfire, leave but ash:
>   In a flash, at a trumpet crash,
> I am all at once what Christ is, since he was what I am, and
> This Jack, joke, poor potsherd, patch, matchwood, immortal diamond,
>   Is immortal diamond.

A. E. HOUSMAN
(1859–1936)

Housman always hoped for a risqué story from me, but it had to be good. Just before he died he was breathing stertorously and was well aware of his imminent death. I thought to divert him by telling him my latest. It concerned the judge affecting ignorance in order to enlighten the jury when the expression 'platinum blonde' arose in court. He asked: 'Am I to understand by "platinum blonde" a precious metal or a common ore?' Housman, between his feeble gasps for air, said: **'That is indeed very good. I shall have to repeat that on the Golden Floor!'** Those were his last words.

R. S. Woods, *Daily Telegraph*, 21 February 1984

Alfred Edward Housman, poet and classical scholar, died in the Evelyn Nursing Home at Cambridge on 30 April 1936. The above account of his final words comes from the physician who had been Housman's doctor for several years before his death.

Woods comments: 'This was an extraordinarily gallant ending for a frail little man'. Housman's reference to the 'Golden Floor' (presumably in heaven) was also somewhat ironic, since he apparently disbelieved in a future life; according to his own account, he became an atheist at the age of twenty-one. His own poem 'For My Funeral' is addressed to a 'thou' whom we may identify with God or a creator, but it views human life as a mere interim in the midst of oblivion:

> We now to peace and darkness
> And earth and thee restore
> Thy creature that thou madest
> And wilt cast forth no more.

Henrik
IBSEN
(1828–1906)

On the contrary!
Michael Meyer, *Henrik Ibsen*, Vol. III (1971)

The Norwegian author whose social plays revolutionized European drama died in Christiania (now Oslo) in the early morning of 23 May 1906. A series of strokes from 1900 onwards had left him largely helpless, unable to write, his mind clear only at intervals.

It has been said that in his last moments Ibsen cried '**No!**', but the weight of evidence is against this. His wife, Suzannah, is reported to have said that he uttered a farewell to her on the night before his death: '**My dear, dear wife, how good and kind you have been to me**'. (It may be remarked that the couple had been married for forty-eight years, but the union had failed to bring Ibsen emotional satisfaction.) The most plausible account, however, states that Ibsen's final word was spoken early in the afternoon of 22 May, in response to a nurse's comment that he seemed to be a little better. Having contradicted her with a single word ('**Tvertimod!**') in his native language, Ibsen lapsed into unconsciousness soon afterwards. Michael Meyer comments: 'It was the last word Ibsen ever spoke; and it came appropriately from one who had devoted his life to the correction of lies'.

Ibsen's ultimate nay-saying contrasts with the end of the Swedish dramatist August Strindberg, whose name is so often coupled with his. Strindberg's personal life had been intensely stormy, with three broken marriages, periods of alcoholism and insanity, and suicide attempts. His onslaughts on religion and conventional morality had led to his standing trial for blasphemy, and his violent diatribes against women, critics, writers and everyone else who was against him roused hostility which only served to heighten his persecution complex. But in his late writing a religious or mystical tone, with themes of forgiveness and redemption, becomes evident; and he died (of cancer of the stomach, in Stockholm, on 14 May 1912) with a Bible clasped to his breast, murmuring '**Everything is atoned for**'.

Thomas Jonathan ('Stonewall') JACKSON
(1824–1863)

In his restless sleep he seemed attempting to speak; and at length said audibly, '**Let us pass over the river, and rest under the shade of the trees**'. These were the last words he uttered. Was his soul wandering back in dreams to the river of his beloved valley, the Shenandoah (the 'river of sparkling waters'), whose verdant meads and groves he had redeemed from the invader, and across whose floods he had so often won his passage through the toils of battle? Or was he reaching forward across the river of Death to the golden streets of the Celestial City, and the trees whose leaves are for the healing of the nations?

R. L. Dabney, *Life of Lieut.-Gen. Thomas J. Jackson*, Vol. II (1866)

'Stonewall' Jackson, the American Confederate general, died on 10 May 1863 near Fredericksburg, Virginia. Barely two years earlier he had been living quietly and obscurely as a professor at the Virginia Military Institute in Lexington, a post he had held since resigning from the army (with the rank of major, and having distinguished himself on active service in Mexico) in 1851. When the Civil War broke out and Virginia seceded from the Union on 17 April 1861, Jackson was commissioned a colonel in the Confederate Army and soon promoted to brigadier-general. He gained his nickname 'Stonewall' for his stern resistance to a Union attack at the first Battle of Bull Run in July, and in October was promoted again, to the rank of major-general. A year later, after a series of military successes demonstrating his wonderful tactical ability and strength of character, Jackson became a lieutenant-general.

On 2 May 1863 at Chancellorsville (near Washington, D.C.), by a brilliant manoeuvre Jackson led his forces to rout Union troops who considerably outnumbered them. At the moment of his greatest triumph, while riding at dusk through his outposts, Jackson was accidentally shot by his own men. He received three wounds, one of which required the amputation of his left arm just below the shoulder. His superior officer, General Robert E. Lee, responded to news of this mishap with a neat compliment: 'You are better off than I am, for while you have lost your left, I have lost my right arm.' But Jackson suffered postoperative complications: pneumonia set in, and he died in delirium after uttering the enigmatic words from which Ernest Hemingway derived the title of his novel *Across the River and into the Trees* (1950). Dabney's interpretation relates to the last two chapters of Revelations, which describe 'the holy city' having a street of pure gold and containing 'the tree of life' with leaves 'for the healing of the nations'.

Henry
JAMES
(1843–1916)

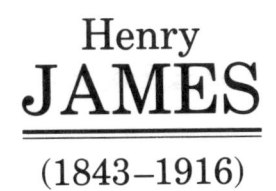

Stay with me, Alice, stay with me.
Leon Edel, *The Life of Henry James: Vol. V,
The Master 1901–1916* (1972)

'So it has come at last – the Distinguished Thing', thought Henry James when he suffered a stroke on 2 December 1915. Typically, he could not name Death directly; it was 'the Distinguished Thing', a theatrical persona, expressed in an utterly Jamesian phrase in which the precise, formal, portentous adjective bumps against the vague, colloquial, and casual noun.

James recovered partially – enough, at least, to enjoy the award of the Order of Merit in the New Year's Honours List of 1916. Having been naturalized as a British subject in July 1915, he had at last become qualified to receive this merited tribute from the country in which he had lived for almost forty years after leaving the United States. Most of his books had proved, in his own words, 'insurmountably unsalable', being too cerebral, evasive, and etiolated for popular taste; but discriminating critics ranked him among the greatest novelists of his time for subtlety, elegance, and insight.

He was also able to resume his habit of dictation. But the words transcribed by his secretary were not altogether lucid. While the style and mode of thought remained characteristic, the subject-matter was more elusive than ever. His thoughts were escaping him, or were not even his thoughts; he seemed to be confusing himself with Napoleon, producing farragoes in which despatches from the French Emperor mingled with the domestic concerns of a timid bachelor writer.

In his flat in Carlyle Mansions, Chelsea, James was nursed by Alice, the widow of his elder brother William (the philosopher who originated the concept of pragmatism and pioneered psychological studies). In conversation with her, as his condition grew worse, Henry James once spoke of his nephews: '**Tell them to follow, to be faithful, to take me seriously.**' On 25 February 1916 he addressed her for the last time, in the words quoted above. Soon afterwards, he lapsed into unconsciousness. On 27 February he tried to speak, but his mutterings were unintelligible. At 6 p.m. on the following day he sighed three times and expired.

JESUS CHRIST
(6? BC–AD 30?)

(a) **Eloi, Eloi, lama sabachthani?** which is, being interpreted, **My God, my God, why hast thou forsaken me?**
Mark 15:34

(b) **Father, into thy hands I commend my spirit.**
Luke 23:46

(c) **It is finished.**
John 19:30

Jesus Christ, the Jewish religious leader considered by his followers to be the incarnate son of God, was crucified at Calvary, outside Jerusalem, at the age of approximately thirty-five.

The date of his death is uncertain: the chronology of the Christian era introduced in the sixth century is definitely faulty, and the most likely date is 7 April 30. The events leading up to his death are likewise clouded by uncertainty. According to the accounts of the four evangelists on whom our knowledge of Christ's life must rely almost entirely, he was condemned to death as a blasphemer by the Jewish supreme court (the Sanhedrin), and the sentence was ratified by Pontius Pilate, the Roman governor of Judea and Samaria. However, other information about affairs in Palestine at the time suggests that this was an unlikely proceeding, and most modern historians believe that he was condemned and executed under Roman law as a political rebel.

The four evangelists offer three distinct versions of Christ's last words on the cross. This discrepancy could perhaps be, at least partly, resolved if we had full information about the composition of the gospels; unfortunately, despite more than a century of modern biblical criticism, their date, authorship, and sources remain uncertain.

The shortest gospel, by Mark, is now generally believed to be the earliest, written some thirty to thirty-five years after Christ's death. The author has traditionally been identified as the Mark who was an associate of St Paul and a companion of St Peter, supposedly a major source of his information about Christ; but this is dubious. Here, Christ's final words (in Aramaic, the Semitic language spoken in Palestine in Christ's time) are a cry of anguish quoting Psalm 22.

Matthew's gospel, written about ten years after Mark's, seems to be largely based on Mark and on a second source which is no longer extant. The identification of the author with Matthew, one of the original twelve disciples, is doubtful. His version of Christ's last utterance (Matthew 27:46) is almost identical to Mark's.

Luke, writing around the year 80, was probably the Luke who was a physician and a companion of St Paul. In his account, Christ's final words quote Psalm 31:5. These words have been echoed in turn by many dying people: for example Charlemagne (742–814), Christopher Columbus (1451–1506), Lady Jane Grey (1537–1554), and Torquato Tasso (1544–1595).

John's gospel, probably written about 100 AD, is the most difficult of all to assess. Some believe the author to be the apostle John, son of Zebedee and younger brother of James, but the evidence is very scanty. John's version of Christ's final words is often quoted in the Latin form

Jesus Christ

'**Consummatum est**'. The translation in the New English Bible, '**It is accomplished**', may be more appropriate than that in the Authorized Version, '**It is finished**', for the former presents Christ's death as the accomplishment of a mission rather than a mere end, and reinforces John's conviction of an irresistible divine purpose fulfilled in Christ's life – a thesis which, on occasion, the author may have determined to illustrate irrespective of whatever historical information was available to him.

It should be added that Christ's last words before death were not the last words he spoke on earth. The Bible tells that he rose from the dead, appeared to his disciples on several occasions, and eventually ascended to heaven. Various reports of his last earthly utterance are given in Matthew 28:18–20, Mark 16:15–18, Luke 24:46–49, and Acts 1:7–8.

Samuel JOHNSON
(1709–1784)

(a) **Jam moriturus! [Now I am about to die!]**
Sir John Hawkins, *The Life of Samuel Johnson* (1787)

(b) While Mrs Gardiner & I were there before the rest came he took a little warm milk in a cup when he said something upon its not being given properly into his hand and I believe that this was the last time he spoke.
John Hoole, *Journal Narrative Relative to Doctor Johnson's Last Illness* (written 1784; edited by O. M. Brack, Jr, 1972)

(c) **God bless you, my dear!**
James Boswell, *The Life of Samuel Johnson* (1791)

The Samuel Johnson that we know best is the figure

presented to us by James Boswell; and we tend to think that every detail of Johnson's life – at least since his meeting with Boswell in 1763 – is faithfully and uniquely recorded in Boswell's biography. As these conflicting accounts of Johnson's death indicate, this may not always be the case: Boswell was the most minute, lively, and artistic of Johnson's biographers, but he was not the first, nor necessarily the most accurate.

Johnson died of dropsy at 7.15 p.m. on 13 December 1784, at his home in Bolt Court, off Fleet Street, London, after several weeks of painful illness. Sir John Hawkins, an acquaintance of Johnson's for over thirty years (despite being described by Johnson as 'a very unclubable man') who was one of his executors and published his *Life and Works* in two volumes in 1787–9, stated that Johnson's last words were addressed to Francesco Sastres, an Italian teacher and translator, who reported them to Hawkins. In this version, Johnson's farewell seems to echo the reputed cry of Roman gladiators: '*Ave, Caesar, morituri te salutant* [*Hail, Caesar, those who are about to die salute you*]'.

A quite different account was given by John Hoole, a translator and dramatist who visited Johnson several times during his last illness. Hoole's version of Johnson's final day begins with a report that the dying man had been visited earlier in the morning by 'Miss Morris (a sister to Miss Morris formerly upon the stage)', who had asked Johnson for his blessing; he had replied 'God bless you!'.

At the time of Johnson's death, James Boswell was in Edinburgh, having left London and Johnson on 30 June. He was not, therefore, an eye-witness of Johnson's death – 'but I had', he adds in his self-centred way, 'the consolation of being informed that he spoke of me on his death-bed with affection' – and his account was avowedly given by him by his brother, Thomas. This narrative seems to be, however, a reworking of Hoole's version, which Boswell acknowledges as one of his sources. It tells how 'a Miss Morris, daughter to a particular friend of his' visited Johnson to ask his blessing and subsequently heard 'the last words he spoke' (but note that Boswell's version of these words adds the phrase 'my dear'). Why Boswell should have ignored the later words which Hoole and Hawkins attribute to Johnson, unless he somehow had good evidence to the contrary, can only be surmised; perhaps he was swayed by notions of artistic effect or by a pious resolution that his hero should die with a benediction, rather than a complaint or a prosaic statement in a dead language, upon his lips.

JUDAS ISCARIOT
(died 30? AD)

Then Judas, which had betrayed him [Christ], when he saw that he was condemned, repented himself, and brought again the thirty pieces of silver to the chief priests and elders, saying, '**I have sinned in that I have betrayed the innocent blood**'. And they said, 'What is that to us? see thou to that'. And he cast down the pieces of silver in the temple, and departed, and went and hanged himself.

Matthew 27:3–5

There is not much certain information that can be gathered from the biblical accounts of Judas. All four evangelists agree that he was one of Christ's twelve disciples, and that he betrayed Christ to the chief priests. Only Matthew specifies that he was paid thirty pieces of silver for this service; and the detail looks suspiciously like an attempt to create a correspondence with an Old Testament prophecy in order to prove that Christ's life was the fulfilment of the scriptures. Judas's motives seem to have been purely mercenary. Matthew says nothing on the point, Mark and Luke state merely that the Devil entered into him, while John indicates his avarice by stating that Judas had embezzled money entrusted to him as treasurer of the disciples.

At the Last Supper, Christ revealed that there was a traitor among the disciples; in the accounts by Matthew and John he specifically named Judas as the man. Subsequently Judas led a body of armed men to Christ in Gethsemane, and identified Christ by kissing him. The gospels of Mark, Luke, and John tell us nothing more about Judas; only Matthew narrates his death on the morning of Christ's crucifixion. However, a rather different story is told in the first chapter of the Acts of the Apostles, traditionally attributed to Luke:

> Now this man purchased a field with the reward of iniquity; and falling headlong, he burst asunder in the midst, and all his bowels gushed out.

This is certainly cryptic, but it seems to imply that Judas's death was caused by a suicidal leap rather than an accidental fall.

Many later legends have accreted around the obscure figure of Judas, not only in Christian writing but also in Coptic and Muslim tradition. A common example relates to the tree on which he supposedly hanged himself. Some accounts identify it as the Judas tree (*Cercis siliquastrum*) – probably because the tree's pinkish-purple flowers, often arising directly from the trunk, could suggest drops of blood. Others say it was the elder (genus *Sambucus*), a tree which, for unknown reasons, has figured in many superstitions. A rival belief holds that Christ's cross was made from the wood of elder.

John
KEATS
(1795–1821)

The approaches of death came on. '**Severn – I – lift me up – I am dying – I shall die easy – don't be frightened – be firm, and thank God it has come!**' I lifted him up in my arms. The phlegm seemed boiling in his throat, and increased until 11, when he

> gradually sunk into death – so quiet – that I still thought he slept.
>
> Joseph Severn, letter to Charles Brown, February 1821

The poet John Keats died of consumption (tuberculosis) on 23 February 1821, in a rented apartment in Rome (26 Piazza di Spagna, now open to the public as the Keats-Shelley Memorial House). In the autumn of 1819 he had begun to exhibit definite signs of consumption, the disease from which his younger brother Tom had died the previous year, and his own medical training made him acutely conscious of the irresistible course of the illness. When he suffered a haemorrhage in the lungs in February 1820, according to an account by his friend Charles Brown he examined the blood he had coughed up and commented calmly: 'I know the colour of that blood; – it is arterial blood; – I cannot be deceived in that colour; – that drop of blood is my death-warrant; – I must die'.

Accompanied by the artist Joseph Severn (1793–1879), in October 1820 Keats left England to spend the winter in Italy. After he had arrived in Rome in November, his condition deteriorated rapidly, causing him to refer pointedly to 'this posthumous life of mine'. Severn, who nursed him devotedly, recorded his final words and arranged for his burial in the Protestant Cemetery at Rome; but although the epitaph on the poet's gravestone followed his own wishes in omitting his name and bearing the inscription 'Here lies one whose name was writ in water', Severn and Brown added a sentimental explanation which spoiled the effect. Although probably filched from Shakespeare – like many of the best things in Keats's poetry – that phrase was at least indicative of his progress towards 'a more thoughtful and quiet power' and a more concentrated and controlled expression. But who can say what creativity Keats's early death curtailed, or how much it has contributed to a high reputation built upon so small an achievement? Can one imagine a middle-aged Victorian Keats, purged of lusciousness and indulgent Romanticism, fulfilling his ambition to write poetry that is 'great and unobtrusive', philosophic, intense, profound, selective, and coherent? Or does one envisage, rather, a fleshy, precious aesthete, penning verses filled with quaint little conceits, archaisms, and elaborate ornaments – perhaps, by now, a man secretly disenchanted with poetry and half in love with an easeful life, calling him soft names in many a musèd rhyme – musèd, forsooth – forever tottering on the brink of bathos?

Ned KELLY

(1855–1880)

Such is life!
Frank Clune, *The Kelly Hunters* (1955)

Edward ('Ned') Kelly was the son of an Irish gamekeeper who was transported to Van Diemen's Land (now Tasmania) for stealing two pigs and who, like many convicts – for they were not given passage back to Britain – stayed in Australia after serving his sentence. Throughout Ned's childhood, members of his feckless family were often in trouble with the law for such offences as horse-stealing, cattle-stealing, assault, and drunkenness. Ned himself was first arrested at the age of fourteen, was in prison twice, and was frequently under observation by the police.

In 1878 Kelly took to the hills with his brother, Daniel, to escape charges (quite possibly trumped up) of shooting at a policeman sent to arrest Daniel for horse-stealing. With two companions, they killed three policemen sent after them and, officially proclaimed outlaws, for nearly two years the four men terrorized Victoria and New South Wales with a series of hold-ups and robberies. Yet, despite the terror, they attracted a considerable amount of popular sympathy. They usually avoided gratuitous violence, never maltreated women, and did not rob the poor; their actions could, perhaps, be blamed on police provocation and incompetence, or on prevailing social conditions. They could be seen – as they still are by some – as romantic figures, the modern equivalent of Robin Hood and his men; or even as class-warriors struggling for the oppressed proletariat against greedy landowners and a repressive government.

In June 1880 the Kelly gang planned to ambush a train carrying police forces as it passed through the township of Glenrowan. For this occasion they created the home-made iron armour which has figured prominently in their legend; but the armour, which hampered their movements and made it difficult for them to shoot accurately, was only one of a series of miscalculations. Surrounded in a hotel, Kelly's colleagues all died. Making a reckless attempt to save them, at sunrise Kelly himself, already badly wounded, staggered in his unwieldy armour into a final magnificently futile combat against more than thirty armed men. Robotically he lurched through the mist towards his enemies, despite a hail of gunfire, until he was overwhelmed and captured, with twenty-eight bullet wounds in his arms and legs.

Brought to trial in October, he was convicted of murder and condemned to death. 'I do not fear death', he said in court: 'I fear it as little as to drink a cup of tea'. On 11 October he was brought to the gallows in Melbourne Jail. As the noose was adjusted round his neck, he said '**Ah well, I suppose it has to come to this!**'; and, as a white cap was pulled down over his head and face, '**Such is life!**'. It has been asserted that he showed cowardice just before his end, but a prison warder who witnessed the execution stated that he 'submitted to his fate without the slightest sign of timidity or fear'.

Hugh
LATIMER
(1485?–1555)

Be of good comfort, Master Ridley, and play the man. We shall this day light such a candle, by God's grace, in England, as (I trust) shall never be put out.
John Foxe, *Acts and Monuments* (5th edition, 1596–7), commonly known as 'Foxe's Book of Martyrs'

Hugh Latimer was not only one of the most influential figures in the Reformation in England, but also an embodiment of a tradition of stubborn individualism and down-to-earth appeal in the English church. A yeoman farmer's son, he never lost his sympathy with the ignorance and sufferings of the poor; in his vivid, homely sermons he lashed social injustice and corrupt clergy; theological subtleties were not his concern, and he never sought power in church or state.

Educated at Cambridge, Latimer was a zealous Papist until he was converted to Protestantism in 1525; he then became so ardent in his new doctrines that in 1532 he was accused of heresy, excommunicated, and briefly imprisoned until he submitted. After Henry VIII had formally repudiated the Pope's authority in 1534, Latimer's influence grew, and in 1535 he was made Bishop of Worcester. When the official religion inclined back towards Roman Catholicism, however, he resigned his see in 1539 over disagreement with the Act of Six Articles which reaffirmed the main Catholic doctrines. Later he again fell under suspicion of heresy and was imprisoned. Although restored to favour by the accession of Edward VI, he declined to resume his bishopric on the grounds that he wished to preach freely without constraint or obligation.

In September 1553, soon after Queen Mary came to the throne, Latimer was arrested. For some time he was confined in the Tower of London; later he was transferred to Oxford, together with Thomas Cranmer (see p. 40) and Nicholas Ridley, Bishop of London. Meanwhile the old statute for the punishment of heretics had been re-enacted, and the execution of John Rogers on 4 February 1555 began the toll of 300 deaths which took place in the next three-and-a-half years. The final hearing of the ecclesiastical commission against Latimer and Ridley took place from 30 September to 1 October 1555. Refusing to recant their opinions, both men were condemned to be degraded from the priesthood and handed over to the secular authorities for execution.

On the morning of 16 October Latimer followed Ridley to the stake erected opposite Balliol College. They made a strange contrasting pair: Ridley, the more sophisticated man, looked dignified in a black gown with fur trimmings, a velvet tippet and nightcap; Latimer wore a threadbare gown of coarse wool, with a large bonnet that buttoned under his chin. When they met at the stake, Ridley reassured his elder colleague: **'Be of good heart, brother, for God will either assuage the fury of the flame or strengthen us to abide it.'** For a few moments they knelt and prayed, then conversed privately. Next, a sermon was preached to them, exhorting them to recant and save themselves. Ridley attempted to answer, but was forbidden. The two men removed their overgarments – whereupon Latimer, who 'in his clothes... appeared a withered and crooked, silly old man... now stood bolt upright, as comely a father as one might behold'.

They were chained to the stake, around which faggots and kindling were heaped. One mercy was allowed them: to hasten their end, small bags of gunpowder were tied round their necks. When the wood was lit, Latimer spoke the famous words quoted above. As the fire flared up, Ridley cried in Latin **'Into your hands, O Lord, I commend my spirit; Lord, receive my spirit'**, repeating the last phrase in English. Latimer responded with the cry **'O Father of Heaven, receive my soul'**; and he 'received the flame as if he were embracing of it. After he had stroked his face with his hands, and as it were bathed them in the fire, he soon died (as it appeared) with very little pain or none'.

In this respect Latimer was more fortunate than his colleague. Around Ridley the fire had been badly laid, so that his agonies were greatly prolonged. **'I cannot burn'**, he cried; **'Lord have mercy upon me – Let the fire come unto me, I cannot burn'**. His brother-in-law's attempts to stoke the fire only made the situation worse; but finally the flames reached the upper part of his body, and set off the gunpowder.

Records show that the total cost of the execution, for materials and labour, was twenty-five shillings and twopence.

Stan
LAUREL
(1890–1965)

I'd rather be skiing than doing this. ['Do you ski, Mr Laurel?' asked a nurse.] **No, but I'd rather be doing that than this.**
Fred Lawrence Guiles, *Stan* (1980)

Arthur Stanley Jefferson was an actor's son, born in Ulverston, Lancashire. He went on the stage as soon as he left school, and in 1910 joined Fred Karno's music-hall troupe, in which Charlie Chaplin was already an established favourite. After touring the USA briefly with this troupe in 1910, Jefferson returned with them in 1912 and decided to stay in that country. For several years he toured in vaudeville; and during this time, because of a superstitious fear of the thirteen letters in the name Stan Jefferson, he changed his surname to Laurel.

Laurel began working in films in 1917, but achieved no great success until, in 1927, the producer Hal Roach inspirationally teamed him with Oliver 'Babe' Hardy. After a few mediocre films in which they found their feet together, they established the mannerisms – bowler hats, ill-fitting clothes, Laurel's whimper and headscratching, Hardy's fiddling with his tie – that served them in numerous successful comedies. Their screen characters complemented each other perfectly: Hardy was the pompous fat man, bland-faced but irritable, a father-figure, always aiming for respectability; Laurel was humble, thin, slow-witted, childlike, always creating chaos.

These qualities of incompetence and innocence were not reflected precisely in Laurel's private life. Incompetent he probably was, as he got himself into one fine mess after another; and perhaps there was a kind of innocence in his nature that made his escapades amoral rather immoral. But on several occasions his career nearly foundered because of his heavy drinking, scandalous womanizing, and stormy relationships with his wives (he married six times, to the same woman on three occasions).

The popularity of Laurel and Hardy declined with changing conditions in the late 1930s. After completing their last film in 1950, they made a few stage appearances, but Hardy suffered increasingly from heart trouble. He died in 1957. Laurel survived him for eight years, dying on 23 February 1965, after a heart attack, at his home in a modest apartment building in Santa Monica, California. With almost his last breath he managed to produce a final – feeble, but stoic – joke.

Saint
LAWRENCE
(died 258)

I am roasted; turn me over and eat.
Saint Ambrose of Milan,
De Officiis Ministrorum (written 386)

Traditional accounts relate that Lawrence was a deacon of Pope Sixtus II at the time of the persecution of Christians by the Roman emperor Valerian. Meeting Sixtus as the Pope was being led away to execution, he was prophetically told: 'Stop weeping; in three days you will follow me'. Lawrence was now ordered by the Roman authorities to hand over the treasures of the Church. He assembled a crowd of diseased, disabled, and elderly people, asserting that these were the Church's real treasures. This equivocal reply was not received favourably, and he was sentenced to be roasted alive on a gridiron. His alleged courageous jest during this cruel martyrdom is reported by several fourth- and fifth-century writers, including St Ambrose, St Augustine, and the poet Prudentius.

While it is generally accepted that this story has an authentic basis, the details of Lawrence's death are doubtful. Probably he was executed by beheading, and the tale of the gridiron derived either from confusion with earlier tales of this punishment or from the lively imagination of hagiographers. It has become, nonetheless, one of the most popular of all the stories of early Christian martyrs, and Lawrence has retained a high status among Christian saints, especially in Italy and Spain. The Basilica of San Lorenzo was built over his tomb in Rome, and the famous El Escorial monastery near Madrid (built in the late sixteenth century) was dedicated to him and, according to some accounts, intended to resemble a gridiron.

John
LENNON
(1940–1980)

I'm shot, I'm shot.
Ray Coleman, *John Ono Lennon: Volume 2, 1967-1980* (1984)

The pop musician John Lennon was killed at 10.50 p.m. on 8 December 1980 in New York. On his return from a recording studio, he was shot five times in the back at the entrance to the exclusive Dakota apartment block in Manhattan where he had lived since 1973. He staggered up some steps to the desk clerk's office, fell on his side, moaned the words quoted above, and died soon afterwards.

The murderer, Mark David Chapman, was a twenty-five-year-old from Georgia who, earlieeer in the day, had obtained Lennon's autograph. His motives have never been explained. Underground rumours hint at a political assassination. Considered subversive by the United States government, Lennon had been under suspicion and surveillance for years. More probably Chapman was just a lost, pained figure. Perhaps he just wanted to become famous – today's instant fame being the spur that raises many murky spirits to shun laborious days – through an outrageous act. After all, Lennon was one of the most famous people in the world – more renowned than any monarch or politician or religious leader or murderer, probably even more than any footballer; had he himself not said that the Beatles were more popular than Jesus Christ? So his killer was certain to attract attention.

But what, one might ask, was the substance beneath the bright aura of Lennon's fame? Sometimes it was hard to distinguish, when his appearance and styles were like the disguises of a quick-change artist. The words of the songs were often snatched out of newspaper headlines, with a touch of facile surrealism and utopianism, some hasty politics, and dollops of sentimentality and self-pity. Not everything, however, was mere image, commercialism, and self-indulgence. Ultimately it is hard to deny the invigorating appeal of that brash, repetitive music and raw, intense but mocking, voice – directly echoing the basic perplexity and semi-inarticulacy of millions from Liverpool, Georgia, or the terminals of the earth.

Queen
MARY I
(1516–1558)

As touching the manner of whose death, some say that she died of a tympany [i.e. swelling of the stomach], some by her much sighing before her death supposed she died of thought and sorrow. Whereupon her council seeing her sighing, and desirous to know the cause, to the end they might minister the more ready consolation unto her, feared (as they said) that she took some thought for the king's majesty, her husband, which was gone from her. To whom she answering again; '**Indeed**' (said she) '**that may be one cause, but that is not the greatest wound that pierceth mine oppressed mind**': but what that was she would not express to them. Albeit afterward she opened the matter more plainly to mistress Rise and mistress Clarentius (if it be true that they told me, which heard it of mistress Rise herself), who then being most familiar with her, and most bold about her, told her that they feared she took thought for King Philip's departing from her. '**Not that only**' (said she) '**but when I am dead and opened, you shall find Calais lying in my heart**'.
Raphael Holinshed,
The Chronicles of England, Scotlande, and Irelande (1577)

Holinshed does not state that Mary's famous phrase was her last speech. Other contemporary sources merely mention her uttering the responses at mass just before her death, which took place between 5 and 6 a.m. on 17 November 1558. Nevertheless, we can accept the above words at least as her summarizing valediction, for it seems likely that the early death of this pious, sincere, and unfortunate queen was hastened by oppressive grief.

First, as Holinshed mentions, there was 'King Philip's departing from her'. Mary had married Philip II of Spain, eleven years her junior, in July 1554. Fourteen months later, on his father's abdication, he went to the Low Countries – whence reports of his debauched behaviour reached England – and, apart from a brief visit in 1557, never returned to his wife. A series of false pregnancies was the most remarkable manifestation of her distress.

In January 1558 the French captured the town of Calais, which had been in English hands since it was won in 1347 by Edward III after nearly a year's siege. Despite repeated warnings of an imminent French attack from 1555 onwards, the town's defences had remained inadequate, and Mary seems to have reproached herself bitterly for this loss of the last significant English stronghold in Europe.

Moreover, Mary's attempt to restore Roman Catholicism in England had cost the lives of 300 Protestant heretics, and earned her the nickname 'Bloody Mary', without winning any popular favour. Childless, abandoned by her husband, conscious of failure, unloved by her subjects, Mary died; whereupon, according to the diarist Henry Machyn, 'all the churches in London did ring, and at night [men] did make bonfires and set tables in the street, and did eat and drink, and made merry for the new queen [Elizabeth]'.

MOLIÈRE
(1622–1673)

> Don't be frightened, you've seen me bring up more [blood] than that. However, go and tell my wife to come up.
>
> J.-L. Le Gallois, Sieur de Grimarest, *La Vie de M. de Molière* (1705; edited by G. Mongrédien, 1955)

A comedian should ideally die on stage, to the sound of the laughter he has provoked – this notion has been commonly expressed after the recent deaths on stage of two popular British comedians, Tommy Cooper and Eric Morecambe. Such a sudden, public, and unsolemn departure may have a peculiar appropriateness; however, the death of the great French comic dramatist and actor Molière (the stage name of Jean-Baptiste Poquelin, an upholsterer's son) had an additional aptness that was savagely ironic.

Late in 1672, when he was already seriously ill with lung disease, Molière wrote his play *Le Malade imaginaire* (known in English as *The Imaginary Invalid* or *The Hypochondriac*). Physicians had often been a target of his wit (as in *Le Médecin malgré lui* and *L'Amour médecin*), but now the satire had a sharper edge: this tale of a hypochondriac named Argan is not only a hilarious exposure of human weakness and the folly of the medical profession, but a desperate attempt to move wild laughter in the throat of death.

The play was first performed at the Palais Royal in Paris on 10 February 1673, with Molière himself playing the role of Argan. On the day of the fourth performance, 17 February, Molière was clearly unwell; but, although friends advised him to cancel the performance, he insisted on going ahead with it for the sake of the theatrical staff, who would receive no wages in the event of a cancellation. He had, however, no illusions about his condition. '**How much a man suffers before dying! But I think it's a good thing that I'm reaching my end**', he said.

Just before the final curtain – after pretending to be a man pretending to be ill – Molière was seized by a convulsion. He managed to get through to the end, and staggered into the dressing-room of his protégé and friend Michel Baron (from whom the biographer Grimarest derived most of his information about Molière's death). There he said: '**The cold is killing me**'. He was quickly taken to his home in the Rue de Richelieu, where, after refusing his wife's soup and eating a small piece of Parmesan cheese with bread, he went to bed. Soon afterwards he suffered a haemorrhage but tried to assure Baron, in the words quoted above, that it was insignificant.

Baron went away to summon Molière's wife, who had gone to another room to fetch a herbal pillow. Left alone with two nuns to whom he was giving lodging, the dramatist died in their arms, according to Grimarest, after expressing 'all the sentiments of a good Christian, and all the resignation which he owed to the will of God'. But even this exemplary deathbed behaviour failed to win him reconciliation with the Church in France. As an actor he was automatically proscribed, and his body was initially refused Christian burial. After several days of controversy, Molière's remains were eventually buried in St Joseph's churchyard on 21 February. The ceremony, which was supposed to take place quietly and privately, was preceded by a virtual riot – but whether this was a demonstration for or against Molière is still not clear. Nor is it certain whether he really was buried in consecrated ground, or in a patch reserved for suicides and stillbirths.

James Scott, Duke of MONMOUTH
(1649–1685)

Prithee, let me feel the axe. – I fear it is not sharp enough.
Elizabeth Doyley, *James, Duke of Monmouth* (1938);
Bryan Bevan, *James Duke of Monmouth* (1973);
J. N. P. Watson, *Captain-General and Rebel Chief* (1979)

James Scott, conceived and born in Holland, was the natural son of King Charles II and Lucy Walter. His father was, at the time of Scott's birth, the exiled son of a recently-executed king, with no certainty of ever regaining his throne; his mother was variously described in contemporary reports as 'a brown, beautiful, bold, but insipid creature' (John Evelyn), as 'a private Welsh woman of no great fame [i.e. reputation] but handsome' (Lord Clarendon), and as one 'who could deny no body' (John Aubrey). Rumours that his father was really not Charles but Colonel Robert Sidney may confidently be discounted; reports that Charles was secretly married to Lucy Walter may have more substance, although Charles always denied them and issued an official statement to this effect in 1679. (Lucy Walter's liaison with Charles was brief, and she died in 1658 at the age of twenty-eight. Charles had no legitimate offspring, although he fathered approximately fourteen children by various mistresses.)

At the age of thirteen Scott was brought to England by his father. Rapidly becoming the King's favourite, he was created Duke of Monmouth in 1663 and received numerous other honours – such as becoming Chancellor of Cambridge University, Commissioner of the Admiralty, and Captain-General of all the armed forces. A weak, pretty, profligate man of no substance, he was soon turned into a popular idol.

On his father's death in 1685 Monmouth claimed the throne,

asserting himself as the true Protestant heir in opposition to Charles's brother, James, who was known as a serious-minded crypto-Papist. For years Monmouth had been the figurehead of politicians plotting to prevent James's succession, and twice Charles had been forced to banish him for his complicity. Returning from exile in the Low Countries, Monmouth landed at Lyme Regis with eighty-two followers on 11 June 1685. He gathered a ragtag army and attacked James's forces at Sedgemoor, near Bridgwater in Somerset, on 6 July. His troops routed, he fled, but was captured two days later in a ditch near Ringwood, Hampshire.

Removed to London, Monmouth reportedly grovelled before James, but was condemned to death for treason and brought to Tower Hill for execution on the morning of 15 July. As he stood on the scaffold, he was cruelly harassed by the sheriffs of London and the bishops of Ely and Bath and Wells, who were determined to exact an abject repentance from him. '**I die very penitent**', he said; '**I die with a clear conscience. I have wronged no man... I will make no speeches. I come to die**.'

He then addressed himself to the details of his beheading. Although this was supposed to be a quick, painless method of execution, it had not always proved reliable. Monmouth was clearly disturbed by reports that a recent victim had been hacked three or four times before dying; for he turned to the executioner, Jack Ketch, and told him '**Do not serve me as you did My Lord Russell**'. He gave Ketch six guineas, with a promise of more money if he did his work well, but added: '**If you strike me twice, I cannot promise you not to stir**'. After lying down and putting his head on the block, he asked to see the axe, tested the edge with his thumb, and commented that it was not sharp enough. Ketch assured him that the axe was sharp enough and heavy enough, yet his first blow merely wounded Monmouth, who turned and looked up at him. The second blow was no more successful; Monmouth made no sound, but crossed his legs. When the third blow also failed, Ketch dropped the axe, shouting 'God damn me, I can do no more. My heart fails me' – but, with the sheriffs threatening him and the crowd yelling for his blood, he resumed his awful work. Accounts differ as to how many further blows he needed, and some even say that he was finally obliged to use a knife to sever Monmouth's head.

Sir John
MOORE
(1761–1809)

I met the General, in the evening of the 16th, being brought in a blanket and sashes. He knew me immediately, though it was almost dark, squeezed me by the hand, and said, '**Anderson, don't leave me**'. He spoke to the surgeons on their examining his wound, but was in such pain he could say little.

After some time, he seemed very anxious to speak to me, and at intervals got out as follows, '**Anderson, you know that I have always wished to die this way**'.

He then asked, '**Are the French beaten?**' which he repeated to everyone he knew, as they came in.

'**I hope the People of England will be satisfied! I hope my Country will do me justice!**' . . .

He then asked Major Colborne, if the French were beaten. And on being told they were on every point, he said, '**It's a great satisfaction for me to know we have beaten the French... I feel myself so strong – I fear I shall be long dying. It is a great uneasiness – It is great pain...**'

He thanked the surgeons for their trouble.

Captains Percy and Stanhope, two of his Aides-de-Camp, then came into the room. He spoke kindly to both, and asked Percy if all his Aides-de-Camp were well. After some interval he said, '**Stanhope – remember me to your sister**'.

He pressed my hand close to his body, and in a few minutes

died without a struggle.
> from an account by Colonel Paul Anderson,
> Moore's closest friend, quoted by Beatrice Brownrigg,
> *The Life and Letters of Sir John Moore* (1923)

Every schoolboy knows – perhaps – about the burial of Sir John Moore at Corunna:

> Not a drum was heard, not a funeral note,
> As his corpse to the rampart we hurried;
> Not a soldier discharged his farewell shot
> O'er the grave where our hero we buried.

One should not take these popular lines, first published anonymously in 1817, too literally. The author was an obscure young Irishman, Charles Wolfe, the curate of Ballyclog, who had no experience of military matters and was inspired by reading a somewhat coloured account of Moore's death and burial.

Other details of Moore's life and death are less well known. He was a dedicated army officer who is credited with greatly improving the morale, discipline, and tactics of the British forces. In various engagements with the French over a period of fifteen years he never shirked from standing in the front line, and suffered a disproportionate number of injuries. In the space of three weeks in Holland in 1799 he had a finger broken by a shot, then was shot through the thigh, then was struck by a shot which entered behind his ear and came out of his cheek under the left eye, and then very nearly killed himself by accidentally drinking a poisonous solution used to dress his wound.

In October 1808 Moore became Commander-in-Chief of the Army in Spain, charged with the task of expelling Napoleon's forces. The mission proved hopeless: he was unable to obtain any significant help from the Spanish, was greatly outnumbered, and could not prevent the gradual disintegration of his army. In terrible weather he marched 250 miles across snow-covered mountainous country to the port of La Coruña (Corunna) to embark his troops. While the transports were coming, the French attacked on 16 January 1809. On horseback, watching the progress of the battle, Moore was struck by a cannon shot which destroyed his left shoulder and part of the collarbone. He was carried into the town, where he died several hours later, and was buried in the ramparts before dawn on the next morning.

Moore's last words were addressed to Captain James Stanhope, a nephew of William Pitt (see p. 136). Moore had been an intimate friend of Pitt and his family, and rumours abounded of a secret engagement between him and Lady Hester Stanhope, Pitt's niece and housekeeper. The truth about this relationship cannot be determined, and it is tempting to read too much into Moore's final utterance: it may have been purely a polite greeting rather than an expression of undying affection. On the other hand, it is reported that Lady Hester, who later achieved notoriety as a traveller in the Middle East and a tiresome virago, devotedly preserved some relics of Moore to the end of her life.

Acrimonious controversy followed Moore's death. His supporters claimed that he had accomplished a brilliant rearguard action in impossible circumstances; his critics held him responsible for a bungled and useless expedition. Corunna can scarcely be considered a victory, for it was essentially similar to the evacuation of the British army from Dunkirk in 1940. Moore's courage and discipline were certainly impressive, but also chilling. Just before he himself was fatally wounded, he coolly admonished a soldier who screamed and writhed unbecomingly after having had his leg shot off: 'My good fellow, don't make such a noise, we must bear these things better.'

Wolfgang Amadeus
MOZART
(1756–1791)

Did I not say that I was writing this Requiem for myself?
F. X. Niemetschek, *Leben des K. K. Kapellmeisters
Wolfgang Gottlieb Mozart* (1798); quoted in Otto Erich Deutsch,
Mozart: A Documentary Biography (1965)

Mozart was taken ill in late autumn 1791, soon after returning to Vienna from a visit to Prague and attending the moderately successful first performance (30 September) of his opera *The Magic Flute*. He took to his bed on 20 November, and died early in the morning of 5 December. Although there was probably nothing very unusual about this untimely death at the age of thirty-five, several sensational legends have been woven around it, particularly regarding the cause of his death and the composition of his *Requiem*.

In the official register of deaths, Mozart's fatal illness was described as 'severe miliary fever' – the epidemic disease commonly known as sweating sickness. Several commentators have believed that the illness was actually typhus fever; others have deduced that Mozart died of an acute kidney disorder, either uraemia or nephritis; but more recent medical research indicates that the ultimate cause of death was heart failure, brought on by an attack of rheumatic fever. But in the very month of Mozart's death a Berlin newspaper reported a rumour that he was poisoned, and there were further more or less cryptic allusions to this story in subsequent years. According to Niemetschek (see below), during his illness Mozart said to his wife: 'My end will not be long in coming: for sure, someone has poisoned me'. Even if this speech is authentic, it does not amount to a direct accusation; it may have been merely a despairing attempt to explain an undiagnosed illness. Towards the end of 1823, however, the rumours burst forth again – and now suspicion pointed in a definite direction. The Italian composer Antonio Salieri (1750–1825), who had become deranged, reportedly confessed that he had poisoned Mozart out of professional jealousy. There is, in truth, no good evidence that Salieri said any such thing; if he did, it was surely either a mad delusion or, at most, a metaphorical reference to his having obstructed Mozart's career through his influence at court. Yet the story seems both indestructible and inspirational: it formed the basis of Rimsky-Korsakov's opera *Mozart and Salieri* (1898), and has recently been revived in Peter Shaffer's play *Amadeus* (1979; filmed in 1984).

Mozart's Requiem Mass in D Minor (K626) was commissioned anonymously, in rather mysterious circumstances, in spring 1791. Mozart worked on it during his final months with great enthusiasm, coupled with a sense of foreboding; the story that he said he felt he was writing his own requiem was widely reported in the years following his death. A rehearsal of sections of the work was sung at his bed on the afternoon of 4 December, with Mozart himself taking the alto part. Niemetschek – author of the first full biography of the composer, containing information from Mozart's widow and generally plausible – states that on the next morning Mozart had the score brought to his bed, looked through it, and uttered the words quoted above. Whether they were strictly his last words is uncertain. Sophie Haibel, Mozart's sister-in-law and a witness to his death, described his final moments thus: 'The last thing he did was to try and mouth the sound of the timpani in his Requiem; I can still hear it now'.

The Requiem, left unfinished by Mozart, was completed by his pupil Franz Xavier Süssmayr – the extent of Süssmayr's contribution is still debated. The work was duly collected on behalf of the man who had commissioned it, but not for nearly a decade was his identity known. Following an appeal from Mozart's widow, he finally revealed himself as Count Franz von Walsegg, an amateur musician who gratified his vanity by ordering works from well-known composers and having them privately performed as his own, and who intended the Requiem to commemorate his late wife. The death of Mozart himself was not honoured in any such way: a few friends attended his short funeral service, but for various reasons none of them accompanied his body to the cemetery, where it was buried in an unmarked common grave.

MUHAMMAD
(570–632)

Nay, the most Exalted Companion is of paradise.
Ibn Isḥāq, *Sīrat Rasūl Allāh* (translated by A. Guillaume as *The Life of Muhammad*, 1955)

Muhammad, the founder of the Islamic religion, lived an unremarkable life as a merchant in the mainly polytheistic society of Arabia until, at the age of forty, he received a vision of the angel Gabriel. Muhammad then began to preach the unity of God and the necessity for repentance, prayer, fasting, and almsgiving. Encountering bitter opposition in Mecca, in 622 with his followers he sought refuge in Medina; this emigration was the celebrated *hijrah* or *hegira* from which the Muhammadan era is dated. From his base in Medina he gradually acquired support, and in 630 entered Mecca triumphantly with 10,000 men. Shortly after returning to Medina from a final pilgrimage to Mecca in April 632, he fell ill, and died on 8 June 632. His death probably resulted from pneumonia, although according to one tradition Muhammad himself claimed the cause was some poisoned lamb served to him by a vengeful Jewish woman three years earlier.

The Qur'an or Koran, the sacred book of Muslims, written down about 650, consists of the revelations given by God to Muhammad. For details of the prophet's life, the primary source is the long biography by Ibn Isḥāq – written in the second half of the eighth century, but, in its extant form, revised by Ibn Hishām early in the ninth century. Ibn Isḥāq's account of Muhammad's death purports to descend by oral tradition from Aisha or Ayesha, who was Muhammad's third wife, the only one who was a virgin when he married her (she was nine years old at the time), and his favourite. (Most of Muhammad's thirteen marriages seem to have been intended to forge links with influential families or to care for distressed widows. Although he was clearly fond of female company, his moral standards were apparently irreproachable.) He spent his last illness in her room, and died in her bosom shortly after cleaning his teeth vigorously with a toothpick.

His final words probably refer to a verse (Surā 4.71) in the Qur'an which describes the good company in paradise enjoyed by obedient men among 'the prophets and the faithful and the witnesses and the upright upon whom Allah hath bestowed favour'. They may, therefore, be taken as a deliberate renunciation of earthly life for the greater joys of heaven.

Another, probably less reliable, tradition states that Muhammad's last words were these: '**O Allah! Pardon my sins. Yes, I come**'. A third version is given in Sir William Muir's *The Life of Muhammad* (1912): '**Lord, grant me pardon; and join me to the companionship on high. – Eternity in Paradise! – Pardon! – The blessed companionship on high!**'

NAPOLEON I

(1769–1821)

France – army – head of the army – Josephine.
Felix Markham, *Napoleon* (1963),
and Vincent Cronin, *Napoleon* (1971)

Napoleon Bonaparte, a Corsican who had become emperor of France and controller of most of continental Europe, abdicated for the second time on 22 June 1815, four days after his defeat at the Battle of Waterloo in Belgium. His first abdication, in the previous year, had led to his exile on the island of Elba in the Mediterranean; but from there he had easily escaped, returned to France, and raised another army to cull the population of France, Britain, and Prussia. Now, his hand forced by French royalists as much as by the victorious Allies, he surrendered to the British on 15 July. 'I come, like Themistocles, to throw myself on the hospitality of the British people,' he declared oratorically in a letter to the Prince Regent, almost as if he were making a generous offer; he could never see himself as other than a victor, and a friend and benefactor to all mankind. Unimpressed by his tattered grandeur, the British government determined to prevent him from initiating any more bloody and economically ruinous wars. Despite Napoleon's protests, the decision was made: he should be exiled to St Helena, a small tropical island in the South Atlantic, over 4000 miles from Europe.

Napoleon disembarked at St Helena in October 1815, accompanied by a few faithful followers and servants. Although a large British military force was established on the island, the terms of his captivity were not, in theory, unduly restrictive. Even in his decline, moreover, he retained such personal magnetism – the very word *chauvinism* derives from one of his uncritically admiring soldiers, Nicolas Chauvin – that he dominated most people who came in contact with him. However, in the British governor, Sir Hudson Lowe, he met a man as intransigent as himself; and the outcome was an unceasing, often petty, hostility between the two, ultimately leading to Napoleon's sulky seclusion in a rat-infested house.

'There seems to have been something in the air of St Helena that blighted exact truth, and he who collates the various narratives on any given point will find strange and hopeless contradictions.' So, quite justifiably, wrote Lord Rosebery (*Napoleon: The Last Phase*, 1900). Certainly there are narratives in abundance: Napoleon himself spent much of his time on the island in dictating self-justifying memoirs, and most of his followers, doctors, and captors have contributed accounts of his last days. But surety on many points concerning Napoleon's death cannot be attained. By the end of 1817 he was showing signs of illness, yet its exact nature has never been proved. Two doctors, an Irishman and an Englishman, were dismissed for giving opinions which Lowe – who thought his captive was shamming – found unacceptable, whereas Napoleon's final doctor, a Corsican named Francesco Antommarchi, was a skilled anatomist but had little experience of dealing with live bodies. Whether the illness was cancer of the stomach or amoebic hepatitis (a liver disease) is not a purely academic question: for if it was the latter, which must have been contracted in the tropical climate of St Helena, then it is possible to blame the British government for his death. Napoleon himself had no doubt: 'I die before my time', he said in his last will, dictated in April 1821, 'killed by the English oligarchy and its hired assassins'. Although the thesis of liver trouble has been upheld mainly by Napoleonists, for political reasons, it is tentatively supported in a recent survey of the evidence by a British physician who seems fundamentally hostile to Napoleon (see Frank Richardson, *Napoleon's Death: An Inquest*, 1974).

Napoleon's death occurred at 5.49 p.m. on 5 May 1821. He had been intermittently delirious for several days, repeatedly enquiring about the relative merits of various drinks and asking what his son's name was (Napoleon II, so-called King of Rome and (later) Duke of Reichstadt, Napoleon's son by his second marriage, became a political pawn after 1815, was greatly distressed by his father's death, and died of tuberculosis at the age of twenty-one). His devoted aide-de-camp (Charles Tristan, Marquis de Montholon) was at his bedside throughout his final night, and it was Montholon who claimed to hear the final disjointed words quoted above, spoken between 3 and 4.30 a.m. Those four broken utterances manage to combine Napoleon's chief preoccupations: his country; his army; his leadership; and his first wife. Joséphine Beauharnais, widow of the executed general Alexandre, Vicomte de Beauharnais, was married to Napoleon in 1796, divorced in 1809 because she failed to bear him a child, and died in 1814; Napoleon's second wife, Marie-Louise of Austria, deserted him while he was in Elba and was living with a lover in Italy at the time of his death.

Napoleon I

Napoleon's body, originally buried in St Helena, was brought back to France in 1840 and given a magnificent funeral in Paris. Despite precautions, some parts of the immortal hero seem to have been surreptitiously removed during the postmortem. His heart and stomach were placed in separate silver vessels; two pieces of intestine were preserved by the Royal College of Surgeons in London until they disappeared during World War II; and a piece of withered flesh purporting to be Napoleon's penis was sold for a large sum at auction in 1969.

Horatio, Viscount NELSON
(1758–1805)

Presently, calling Hardy back, he said to him in a low voice, '**Don't throw me overboard**'; and he desired that he might be buried by his parents, unless it should please the king to order otherwise. Then reverting to private feelings, '**Take care of my dear Lady Hamilton, Hardy. Take care of poor Lady Hamilton – Kiss me, Hardy**', said he. Hardy knelt down and kissed his cheek: and Nelson said, '**Now I am satisfied. Thank God I have done my duty**'. Hardy stood over him in silence for a moment or two, then knelt again and kissed his forehead. '**Who is that?**' said Nelson; and being informed, he replied, '**God bless you, Hardy**'. And Hardy then left him – for ever.

Nelson now desired to be turned upon his right side, and said, '**I wish I had not left the deck; for I shall soon be gone**'. Death was, indeed, rapidly approaching. He said to the chaplain, '**Doctor, I have not been a great sinner**': and after a short pause, '**Remember that I leave Lady Hamilton and my daughter Horatia as a legacy to my country**'. His articulation now became difficult; but he was distinctly heard to say, '**Thank

God, I have done my duty'. These words he repeatedly pronounced; and they were the last words which he uttered. He expired at thirty minutes after four, – three hours and a quarter after he had received his wound.

    Robert Southey, *The Life of Nelson* (revised edition, 1830)

The Battle of Trafalgar was fought on 21 October 1805 off the southwest coast of Spain, near the entrance to the Straits of Gibraltar. On one side were twenty-seven British ships; on the other, thirty-three French and Spanish vessels. The battle, which began at midday and ended about five, was a decisive British victory which dashed Napoleon's last hopes of invading Britain: eighteen French and Spanish ships were captured, and four of those which escaped were taken soon afterwards.

At 1.15 p.m. Admiral Nelson, while on the deck of his flagship, the *Victory*, was struck by a sniper's shot from the *Redoutable*. Passing through his shoulder and chest, the bullet broke his spine. '**They have done for me at last, Hardy**', he commented. He was carried below to the cockpit, where his wound was examined and pronounced fatal. There he lay while the battle raged, with Hardy coming in twice to report successful progress.

To the full account of his last hours given above, only some brief notes need be added.

(1) Nelson's request not to be thrown overboard was heeded; his body was brought back to England in the *Victory*, and a splendid funeral was held in St Paul's Cathedral.

(2) Emma, Lady Hamilton (1765–1815), became Nelson's mistress in 1798. The liaison attracted scandal because both were married: he to Frances Nisbet, she to Sir William Hamilton, British envoy to the Kingdom of Naples. After Nelson's death she was ignored by the nation, fell heavily into debt, and died almost destitute in Calais. In 1801 she bore Nelson a daughter, Horatia, who married a Norfolk clergyman and lived until 1881.

(3) Thomas Masterman Hardy (1769–1839), captain of the

Victory from 1803, had served several times previously under Nelson. He was created a baronet in 1806 and rose to the rank of vice-admiral. Nelson's request for a kiss from Hardy need not be considered unusual; there is evidence that this was an accepted method of salutation between men. The theory that Nelson really said '*Kismet* [i.e. Fate], *Hardy*' is not to be taken seriously.

(4) Nelson's final words echo his famous signal to the fleet on the morning of the battle: 'England expects that every man will do his duty.' Having originally dictated 'England confides...', he was persuaded to modify it for convenience in signalling.

Most of our information about Nelson's death derives from the account by William Beatty, surgeon on the *Victory*. His narrative was used by Clarke and McArthur, authors of a painstaking but inelegant biography of Nelson (1809), which in turn formed the basis of Robert Southey's more readable work.

NERO
(37–68)

Too late... This is loyalty!
Suetonius, 'Nero', *Lives of the Caesars* (written *ca* 120)

Nero Claudius Caesar, the fifth emperor of Rome, killed himself on 9 June 68, after ruling for fourteen years. A revolt against him, begun in Gaul and Spain, had spread through the Roman army. Deserted even by his bodyguard, Nero fled in confusion and terror to the house of a freedman four miles outside Rome. There he received news that the Senate had proclaimed Galba as emperor and had condemned Nero to death by flogging with rods. To avoid this ignominy, with the help of his secretary he stabbed himself in the throat.

Immediately afterwards a centurion, one of a group of cavalry sent with orders to take Nero alive, came in and attempted to staunch the wound with his cloak. Nero, believing that the soldier was trying to rescue him, exclaimed – perhaps ironically – at the man's loyalty. After his death, such signs of terror remained in his fixed and staring eyes that his corpse horrified everyone who saw it.

A much more famous final statement is usually attributed to Nero: '**Qualis artifex pereo!** [**What a great artist dies in me!**]' – a reference to his pretensions as a singer, lyre-player, and actor, which had led him to undertake a triumphant tour of Greece and Italy, carrying off the first prize at every competition he entered (and also at the competitions which he did not enter). But Suetonius, our only early authority for the details of Nero's death, plainly states that Nero made several comments after these words.

The rather obscure circumstances of Nero's end gave rise to strange rumours. Between the years 69 and 88 three impostors claiming to be Nero appeared in Greece and Asia Minor; and, around the end of the first century, the Greek writer Dio Chrysostom reported that 'many actually think he is still alive'.

It may be doubted, admittedly, whether we should believe all that we read about Nero in the pages of early writers, let alone in the legends disseminated in medieval times. Even his worse critics tend to admit that, although dissipated, he ruled mildly and reasonably for several years. Then, in 59, he had his mother, Agrippina, the dominating influence over his life, put to death. According to Tacitus she cried '**Strike here!**' – pointing to her womb – to the assassins sent by her son. From that point, Nero allegedly threw off all restraints. For example, he caused the deaths of his first two wives: Octavia was divorced, banished, and murdered, and he killed Poppaea Sabina – of whom he seems to have been genuinely fond – by kicking her in a fit of anger while she was pregnant. Nero later married Statilia Messalina, who rather surprisingly survived him; according to Suetonius he also went through a marriage ceremony with a boy named Sporus.

Suetonius, Tacitus, and Cassius Dio all allege that he sang while Rome burned in 64 BC; but it is now thought unlikely that he was responsible for this fire which ravaged three-quarters of the city, and the cause and extent of his subsequent persecution of Christians are both open to debate.

Tales of Nero's vice, cruelty, and dementia are numerous, and sometimes barely credible. Recent historians, re-examining the early sources critically, have interpreted him rather more sympathetically. Some have produced revisionist accounts arguing that he has been greatly maligned and misunderstood; in his provocatively-titled work *Saint Néron* (1961), Jean-Charles Pichon even suggests that Nero was secretly a Christian, converted by St Paul.

Sir Isaac NEWTON
(1642–1727)

I do not know what I may appear to the world, but to myself I seem to have been only like a boy playing on the seashore, and diverting myself in now and then finding a smoother pebble or a prettier shell than ordinary, whilst the great ocean of truth lay all undiscovered before me.

manuscript by John Conduitt; see Louis Trenchard More, *Isaac Newton* (1934), and Frank E. Manuel, *A Portrait of Isaac Newton* (1968)

These words of a great scientist and mathematician were recorded by John Conduitt (1688–1737), who married Newton's niece in 1717, succeeded Newton as Master of the Mint in 1727, and collected materials for a projected biography of Newton. Whether they were strictly Newton's last words may be doubted; Conduitt states merely that they were uttered shortly before his death, which took place early in the morning of 20 March 1727 at Newton's home in Kensington. They are, however, surely more trustworthy than the two other well-known anecdotes about Newton: the story of a dog destroying his manuscripts is very dubious, while the tale of a falling apple suggesting to him his theory of gravity has been, at the least, embroidered.

The memorable humility in these words was not a quality characteristic of Newton during most of his busy and disputatious career. Discovering the binomial theorem, differential and integral calculus, and the law of universal gravity, constructing the first reflecting telescope, solving many other problems in mathematics and optics, writing on astronomy and theology – even such achievements finally appeared to him as mere diversions on the shore of 'the great ocean of truth'.

Newton's words may contain a reminiscence of lines in Book IV of John Milton's *Paradise Regained*, where an indiscriminate reader is compared to 'children gathering pebbles on the shore'. In turn, his imagery of the sea is closely, but presumably unintentionally, echoed in two poetic tributes to him. First, in James Thomson's 'To the Memory of Sir Isaac Newton', written just after Newton's death:

> The noiseless tide of time, all bearing down
> To vast eternity's unbounded sea,
> Where the green islands of the happy shine,
> He stemmed alone.

Secondly, in William Wordsworth's more famous reference (*The Prelude*, Book III), perhaps influenced by Thomson's lines, to the statue of Newton in the antechapel of Trinity College, Cambridge:

> The marble index of a mind for ever
> Voyaging through strange seas of thought, alone.

Lawrence
OATES
(1880–1912)

I am just going outside and may be some time.
R. F. Scott, *Journal*, 16/17 March 1912

Lawrence Edward Grace Oates, nicknamed Titus, was an officer in the Inniskilling Dragoons when he joined the Antarctic expedition commanded by Captain R. F. Scott. The expedition set out from Britain in June 1910, arrived in New Zealand in October, and reached McMurdo Sound by the end of the year. Early in January 1912 Scott, Oates, and three companions – Dr E. A. Wilson, Lieutenant H. R. Bowers, and Petty Officer Edgar Evans – set off by sledge on the final stages of their journey to the South Pole. Arriving at the Pole on 17 January, they found to their dismay that the Norwegian explorer Roald Amundsen had beaten them to their goal by a month.

Their return journey was slow, in terrible weather. Evans died as the result of a fall, and Oates, crippled by frostbite and recognizing that their food supply was running low, determined to sacrifice his own slim chance of survival. Awaking one morning in the tent where the four survivors were pinned by a blizzard, he spoke his final words and walked outside. Later searches failed to find any trace of him.

Scott wrote: 'We knew that poor Oates was walking to his death, but though we tried to dissuade him, we knew it was the act of a brave man and an English gentleman. We all hope to meet the end with a similar spirit, and assuredly the end is not far' (see p. 159).

Charles Stewart
PARNELL
(1846–1891)

Late in the evening he suddenly opened his eyes and said: **'Kiss me, sweet Wifie, and I will try to sleep a little'**. I lay down by his side, and kissed the burning lips he pressed to mine for the last time. The fire of them, fierce beyond any I had ever felt, even in his most loving moods, startled me, and as I slipped my hand from under his head he gave a little sigh and became unconscious. The doctor came at once, but... my husband died without regaining consciousness, before his last kiss was cold on my lips.

Katharine O'Shea, *Charles Stewart Parnell* (1914)

Charles Stewart Parnell met Katharine O'Shea in 1880. She was the daughter of the late Sir John Page Wood (chaplain to George IV's wife, Queen Caroline), and the wife of William O'Shea, a former military officer sitting as MP for County Clare. Parnell was president of the Irish National Land League, MP for the City of Cork, and chairman of the Irish Parliamentary Party: a man of enormous influence, popularly known as 'the uncrowned king of Ireland'. A passionate liaison between the two began almost immediately – initially, it would seem, with the connivance of her ambitious husband. By 1881 Parnell was writing to her as 'My own Wifie', and early in 1882, while he was imprisoned on political grounds, she gave birth to his daughter – but the child died very soon after.

In the mid-1880s O'Shea contemplated divorce proceedings, but delayed in the hope of gaining a legacy from a rich elderly aunt of his wife. Parnell, meanwhile, was struggling to extricate himself from the scandal of his alleged approbation of the murders of the Chief Secretary of Ireland and Permanent Under-secretary in Phoenix Park, Dublin, in May 1882. Eventually he was vindicated by a special commission appointed by Parliament, after an Irish journalist named Richard Pigott had confessed to forging the two letters bearing Parnell's name which had given rise to accusations of his involvement in the assassinations. But an even more damaging scandal followed in 1890 when Captain O'Shea sued for divorce, citing Parnell as co-respondent, and won his case. The taint of adultery ruined Parnell. Condemned by the Church and many of his former supporters, deposed as chairman of his party, maligned and assaulted, he tried in vain to restore his public life. He married Katharine O'Shea on 25 June 1891 but died of rheumatic fever in Brighton only a few months later – just before midnight on 6 October.

Immediately after Parnell's death, it was reported in the press that his last words had been: '**Let my love be given to my colleagues and to the Irish people**'. If those words sound suspiciously pat and rhetorical, on the other hand his widow's account looks unpromisingly pious and sentimental. Although her novelettish style may prejudice us, a recent biographer is convinced that her narrative is true: 'When his widow indignantly repudiated the legend and insisted that the murmured endearment was what he really said, both her sincerity and the fact that the words themselves, like so many of their intimacies, trembled on the edge of bathos, compel the belief that she spoke the truth' (F. S. L. Lyons, *Charles Stewart Parnell*, 1977).

Anna
PAVLOVA
(1885–1931)

Get my Swan costume ready.
Oleg Kerensky, *Anna Pavlova* (1973)

Anna Pavlova, the Russian-born foremost ballerina of her time, died early in the morning of 23 January 1931. Several days previously, the train on which she had been travelling from Cannes to Paris collided – not seriously – with a goods train. Leaving the train to see what was happening, Pavlova caught a chill from the night air, and pneumonia developed. She continued her journey to the Hague, where she was due to start a European tour – she had toured widely and incessantly since resigning her position as prima ballerina of the Imperial Ballet in 1913 – but there she took to her bed in the Hotel des Indes. Her condition became grave; on the evening of 22 January she lost consciousness, awoke briefly to whisper to her maid the words quoted above, but died half an hour later.

Pavlova's most famous balletic role was *The Dying Swan* (or *The Swan*), a solo created for her in 1907 by her compatriot Michel Fokine, to music by Camille Saint-Saëns. Her final reference to this piece may have been delirious, but it was not inappropriate: the dance depicts a swan's brave but futile struggle for life, ending with its death-tremors.

Spencer
PERCEVAL
(1762–1812)

I am murdered, murdered!
Denis Gray, *Spencer Perceval* (1963)

At 5.15 p.m. on 11 May 1812 the Prime Minister hastened into the lobby of the Houses of Parliament at Westminster. As he entered, a stranger stepped forward and shot him, virtually at point-blank range, in the chest. Spencer Perceval staggered forward, made a muffled exclamation, and fell on his face at the feet of William Smith, MP for Norwich. Carried into an antechamber, he groaned twice before dying.

There are differing reports of Perceval's last utterance. William Smith's own account gives the words quoted above. A contemporary print shows him speaking the single word '**Murder!**', while other narratives say that he muttered '**O God!**' or '**O my God!**'. In any case, it was a simple shocked outcry, which is scarcely surprising. Perceval is the only British Prime Minister to have been assassinated, and one of the least likely to have suffered this fate. Well-intentioned and weak, he was not the sort of man who made mortal enemies. After training as a lawyer and rising in politics through his contacts with William Pitt, when he became Prime Minister in 1809 he presided over one of the most anonymous and untalented cabinets ever raked together. The virtues and limitations of this man were summed up by his contemporary Lord Brougham:

> A man of very quick parts, much energy of character, dauntless courage joined to patient industry, practised fluency as a speaker, great skill and readiness as a debater; but of no information beyond what a classical education gives the common run of English youths. Of views upon all things the most narrow, upon religious and even politi-

cal questions the most bigoted and intolerant, his range of mental vision was confined in proportion to his ignorance on all general subjects.

Poor Perceval could neither have foreseen nor prevented his death. His assassin, who made no attempt to escape after the deed, was a bankrupt merchant named John Bellingham whose life had been an almost complete series of misfortunes. Some years earlier, while on business in St Petersburg, he had been ill-treated and abused by the Russian authorities. His repeated attempts to obtain redress from the British government had failed; and now, embittered and almost certainly deranged, he had decided to take revenge. He had no political motive, and had not even fixed on Perceval as his target – Leveson-Gower, British ambassador in St Petersburg at the time of his troubles, would have sufficed him – but the unfortunate Prime Minister happened to appear first and experienced a death which, rather than any of his previous doings, at least entitled him to a footnote in history.

Within a week Bellingham was tried and hanged. His deed was so unBritish, and smacked of such gross insubordination if not of unthinkable revolution, that the whole affair had to be swept away as soon as possible.

PERICLES

(495?–429 BC)

No Athenian ever wore mourning because of me.
Plutarch, *Life of Pericles* (written *ca* 120)

The Greek biographer Plutarch paints a memorable, but slightly puzzling, portrait of the last moments of the Athenian statesman Pericles. While Pericles lay dying of the plague which ravaged Athens in 429 BC, his friends gathered round his deathbed and discussed his character, virtues, exploits, and military triumphs. They thought that he could no longer hear or speak; but he suddenly joined in the discussion, pointing out that his triumphs depended merely on fortune, whereas his greatest claim to renown was this – '**No Athenian ever wore mourning because of me**'.

This is a surprising assertion from the lips of a military leader and imperialist. Pericles was, in the words of the contemporary historian Thucydides, 'the most powerful man of his time', and considerable bloodshed could be blamed on him. In his efforts to make Athens the political and cultural leader of Greece he had led many soldiers to death, and it was his intransigent attitude towards the Spartans that contributed to the outbreak in 431 BC of the disastrous Peloponnesian War which dragged on for almost thirty years, cost many lives, and ultimately ruined Athens.

Yet Pericles' final words were not altogether an empty boast. His meaning is perhaps to be explained by another comment from Plutarch: 'He himself accounted it his greatest virtue that he never gave way to feelings of envy or hatred'. His motives were always state policy, rather than a desire for personal enrichment or aggrandizement (in planning the Peloponnesian War he viewed life as much more important than property – an opinion that did not find favour among landowners whose estates were abandoned to Spartan pillage), and he apparently treated his political enemies with unusual leniency.

PHEIDIPPIDES

(died 490? BC)

> Rejoice, we win.
> Lucian of Samosata, *Pro Lapsu inter Salutandum*
> (*On a Slip in Greeting*)

One of the best-known tales from Greek history is that of the soldier who ran from the battlefield of Marathon to Athens, a distance of about twenty-five miles, to bring news of a great victory. In September 490 BC a force of 9000 Athenians and 1000 Plataeans routed a much greater army (variously estimated at between 25,000 and 50,000 men) sent by Darius, King of Persia, to punish the Athenians for their incursions into Asia and to restore the deposed tyrant Hippias to control of Athens.

The story of this heroic run has given the English language the word *marathon* to describe a long-distance race (and, by extension, any feat of endurance), and has generally been taken as a historical fact. Unfortunately, the evidence for it is dubious. The earliest account seems to be that of Lucian, the second-century writer, who merely refers briefly to Philippides, a dispatch-runner, bringing the news of Marathon to Athens, and dying immediately he had delivered his message. Now, Lucian was not a historian but a satirical essayist, and he mentions Philippides merely as part of his attempt to trace the origin of the Greek greeting *Chairete* (*Rejoice*). He was writing, moreover, almost 700 years after the Battle of Marathon. Where he got the story from remains uncertain: he may have been following oral tradition, or the work of some writer no longer known to us, or he may have confused the available facts.

For detailed information about the Battle of Marathon we are dependent on the account of Herodotus, the Greek historian writing some fifty years after the event. Herodotus says nothing about any runner being sent to Athens with news of the battle; in his narrative, immediately after the

Pheidippides

battle the whole Athenian army made a forced march back to the city to defend it. He does, however, tell a tale of an even more remarkable run. According to Herodotus, at the news of the Persian approach the Athenians sent a messenger to Sparta to ask for help. This messenger, a professional long-distance runner named Pheidippides, arrived at Sparta – about 140 miles distant from Athens, across rough country – the day after leaving. His main mission failed; for the Spartans, although willing to help, were prevented by religious law from sending an army until the moon was full. (A Spartan army did eventually arrive at Marathon, just in time to inspect the dead bodies and congratulate the Athenians.) He returned, nonetheless, with good tidings, stating that on his way he had met the god Pan. Pan complained that the Athenians neglected him, but promised them his protection if they paid observances to him.

The first modern Olympic Games, at Athens in 1896, included a long-distance race (appropriately won by a Greek runner); it was called the Marathon. The current standardized distance for the race, 26 miles 385 yards, was first used in the 1908 Olympics in London. But, if we believe a fairly plausible historian rather than an obscure tradition, then modern athletes truly wishing to emulate Pheidippides ought to run more than five times that distance.

Pablo
PICASSO
(1881–1973)

You are wrong not to marry. It's useful.
Patrick O'Brian, *Pablo Ruiz Picasso* (1976)

The most renowned and influential of twentieth-century artists died at his home in Mougins in the South of France on 8 April 1973. The cardiologist who had come to attend him during his final illness was a bachelor, and it was to him that Picasso addressed his last words while stretching out a hand to his wife, Jacqueline.

Picasso married twice. His first wife was a dancer, Olga Koklova, the daughter of a Russian colonel; he met her during his association with Sergey Diaghilev's Russian Ballet, for which he designed several sets between 1917 and 1924. This marriage took place in 1918 and was dissolved in 1935. When he was nearly eighty Picasso married Jacqueline Roque, a Frenchwoman more than forty years younger than himself.

Picasso's creativity was closely linked to his relationship with women who were his models and muses. The state of marriage, however, did not always seem to be a necessity. Ironically, Picasso's wives have attracted less attention than his mistresses; these included Fernande Olivier, Marcelle Humbert ('Eva'), Marie-Thérèse Walter (who bore him one child), Dora Maar, and Françoise Gilot (who bore him two children, and disconcerted the painter by publishing her intimate memoir *Life with Picasso* in 1964).

William
PITT
(1759–1806)

(a) **Oh, my country! How I love my country!**
Earl Stanhope, *Life of William Pitt* (1862)

(b) **Oh, my country! How I leave my country!**
Earl Stanhope, *Life of William Pitt* (1879)

(c) **My country! Oh, my country!**
George Rose, *Diaries and Correspondence*
(edited by L. V. Harcourt, 1860), 23 January 1806

(d) **I am sorry to leave the country in such a situation**.
George Canning, letter to Granville Leveson Gower,
29 January 1806, in *Lord Granville Leveson Gower
(First Earl Granville): Private Correspondence 1781–1821*,
edited by Castalia Countess Granville (1916)

(e) He said smilingly: '**Remember, I die in peace with all men – public and private**'. After that, extreme weakness made his voice hardly audible. Amongst the last things that were heard, and which he made an effort to say, was that he had nothing to bequeathe, but that if a life devoted and worn out in the service of his country was thought worthy of any remuneration, he wish'd that country to recollect he left two nephews and a niece in absolute Beggary.
Henrietta, Countess of Bessborough,
letter to Granville Leveson Gower,
23 January 1806, in *Granville... Correspondence*, as (d)

(f) **I think I could eat one of Bellamy's veal pies**.
from an account by Benjamin Disraeli;
see Robin Reilly, *Pitt the Younger* (1978),
and E. Royston Pike, *Britain's Prime Ministers* (1969)

An unprepossessing and rather unapproachable man: inelegant in appearance, cold in manner, extremely shy, apparently celibate, with few friends or amusements and no conspicuous vices except a fondness for port wine; outside his political life, Pitt was something of an odd and ineffectual fish. But in his role as a statesman he was transformed: fluent and spellbinding as an orator, bold and dedicated as an administrator. Following his father (William Pitt, Earl of Chatham) into politics in 1780, he rose meteorically to power and became Prime Minister at the age of twenty-four. Although his opponents initially scorned this unlikely appointment, he succeeded in holding office continuously for seventeen years—the longest consecutive reign of any British premier except for Sir Robert Walpole – and, after three years out of office, in 1804 formed a second government which lasted until his death. His record as Prime Minister was not unblemished – military disasters abroad and oppression at home can be laid at his door – but of his integrity and patriotism there can be no doubt.

Pitt's health was failing by 1805. He made his last speech on 9 November at the Guildhall in London, when the Lord Mayor toasted him as 'the saviour of Europe'. But Europe seemed reluctant to be saved, and news from the continent continued to harass him; Napoleon's victory over the Austrians and Prussians in December occasioned Pitt's famous remark 'Roll up that map; it will not be wanted these ten years', and gave him a shock from which he never recovered. He died at his home in Putney on 23 January 1806, after a period of delirium in which he had been summoning invisible messengers and taking part in imaginary parliamentary debates.

Accounts of Pitt's last words are such a tissue of contradiction and confusion that one almost despairs of the human ability to record any fact accurately and objectively. The primary source is – or should be – a manuscript account of Pitt's death written, just a few days after the event, by his nephew, James Hamilton Stanhope. This account was used in the semi-official biography of Pitt by Philip Henry Stanhope, James's nephew. Alas, a small but crucial discrepancy ruins its value.

In the 1862 edition of Stanhope's work, Pitt loves his country; in the revised 1879 edition, he merely leaves his country. It looks as if Stanhope was aware of the discrepancy, and was willing to explain it, for in the 1879 edition the wording is keyed to a footnote asking the reader to 'See note B at the end of the volume' – which looks promising until one discovers that no notes whatsoever are to be found at the end of the volume.

Another version – similar, but avoiding any mention of either 'love' or 'leave' – was recorded by the statesman George Rose (1744–1818), who served in various capacities during both Pitt's ministries. But Rose's account was rejected by George Canning (1770–1827), another of Pitt's ministers, who asserted that it was 'an expression wholly unlike his usual simplicity of character' and provided another version.

The Countess of Bessborough derived her narrative from Sir Walter Farquhar, one of the physicians attending Pitt. This account is of a wholly different nature, but it is very plausible. Pitt was overwhelmed by debts – although far from extravagant, he made little money from his political career and was careless about his domestic expenses – so it seems natural that he should have been anxious on this point. In the event, after his death the House of Commons paid off all his debts and awarded a substantial pension to his young relatives; among them was his niece, Lady Hester Stanhope (1766–1839), who kept house for him in the last years of his life and was rumoured to be the fiancée of Sir John Moore (see page 113).

Finally, there is the celebrated anecdote of Pitt's sudden craving for a pie. This story comes from Benjamin Disraeli; he claimed that it was told to him by an elderly servant at the House of Commons, who said that he had been summoned late one night to bring pies to Pitt, but had found the statesman dead when he arrived. This may be true, but it does not sound very convincing; perhaps Disraeli had his leg pulled, or perhaps he was trying to debunk the noble final sentiments commonly attributed to his great predecessor.

Edgar Allan
POE
(1809–1849)

Lord help my poor soul!
Hervey Allen, *Israfel: The Life and Times of
Edgar Allan Poe* (1927),
and Edward Wagenknecht, *Edgar Allan Poe* (1963)

The death of Poe was as grotesque and mysterious as any of his fictions. Certainly, the course of his whole life rarely ran smooth or clear. His education at Stoke Newington, of all unlikely places – his turbulent relationship with his foster father – his enlistment in the US army under the name Edgar A. Perry – his expulsion from the military academy at West Point for gross (and apparently deliberate) neglect of duty – his marriage to his cousin Virginia Clemm, thirteen years old at the time although the marriage certificate falsely described her as twenty-one – her early death from tuberculosis – his intemperance and erratic behaviour – such events may seem to belong to legend rather than to recent history, yet his end outdid them all in strangeness.

On 27 September 1849 Poe left Richmond, Virginia, apparently intending to travel to Philadelphia. But what happened to him during the next few days remains, despite the thorough researches of several biographers, almost a complete mystery. The next ascertainable fact is that on 3 October Dr J. E. Snodgrass, a physician in Baltimore vaguely acquainted with Poe, received a note from a local compositor informing him that he had found (lying in the street) 'a gentleman, rather the worse for wear ... who goes under the cognomen of Edgar A. Poe, and who appears in great distress'.

Snodgrass, hastening to meet Poe, found him semi-conscious and dressed in clothes not his own. Poe was taken to the Washington College Hospital in Baltimore, where he recovered consciousness; but he was quite unable to explain his condition. It may simply be that he had succumbed, not for the first time, to alcohol. Or, when in a drunken or emotional state, he may have been drugged and taken from poll to poll to vote in an election – a practice by no means unknown.

Later, Poe became delirious. Throughout one night he kept shouting the name '**Reynolds**', which is also something of a mystery. He may have been thinking of Jeremiah Reynolds, whose project for exploring the South Polar seas had been one of the inspirations for Poe's novel *The Narrative of Arthur Gordon Pym* (1838). But, if the theory that he was a victim of electoral skulduggery is correct, he may possibly have been referring to Henry R. Reynolds, one of the election judges.

Poe died about 5 a.m. on 7 October. His last words, quoted above, are recorded in a letter from J. J. Moran, a doctor at the hospital, to Poe's aunt and mother-in-law, Mrs Maria Clemm. Even here, however, the story is doubtful; the words are so commonplace and unlike Poe that there is some suspicion that Moran created them out of a pious wish to assure a grieving relative that Poe died in a peaceful and Christian fashion.

POMPEY

(105–48 BC)

As it was a considerable distance to the land from the galley, and none of those in the boat addressed any friendly conversation to him, looking at Septimius he said, '**I am not mistaken I think in recognizing you as an old comrade of mine**'; and Septimius nodded without making any reply or friendly acknowledgment. As there was again a profound silence, Pompeius who had a small roll on which he had written a speech in Greek that he intended to address to Ptolemaeus, began reading it. As they neared the land, Cornelia with her friends in great anxiety was watching the result from the galley, and she began to have good hopes when she saw some of the king's people collecting together at the landing as if to honour Pompeius and give him a reception. In the mean time, while Pompeius was taking the hand of Philippus that he might rise more easily, Septimius from behind was the first to transfix him with his sword; and Salvius, and after him Achillas drew their swords. Pompeius drawing his toga close with both hands over his face, without saying or doing anything unworthy of himself, but giving a groan only, submitted to the blows, being sixty years of age save one, and ending his life just one day after his birthday.

Plutarch, *Life of Pompey* (written *ca* 120; translated by George Long)

Gnaeus Pompeius Magnus, 'Pompey the Great', co-ruler of the Roman world with Crassus and Caesar from 60 to 54 BC, was defeated by Caesar in the civil war of 49-48 BC.

Escaping the rout of his troops at Pharsalus in Thessaly, Pompey decided to seek refuge in Egypt, where the thirteen-year-old king, Ptolemy XII, was under certain obligations to him. He therefore set sail from Cyprus, sending ahead a messenger to Ptolemy to announce his arrival. This news, however, put the Egyptians in a dilemma. If they welcomed Pompey, they would anger Caesar; if they refused to harbour him, they would not only make an enemy of Pompey – whose fleet was still powerful – but also annoy Caesar by forcing him to pursue Pompey elsewhere. At a meeting of the young king's advisers, the unscrupulous opinion of one Theodotus, a teacher of rhetoric, prevailed: that they should invite Pompey to Egypt, but kill him at once – for, Theodotus said with a smile, 'A dead man does not bite'.

Pompey's companions, and his wife Cornelia, were well aware of the possibility of deceit. They warned Pompey, and watched with foreboding as he was taken from his ship, lying offshore at Pelusium, in an Egyptian fishing-boat. The boat contained Achillas (one of the king's advisers), a centurion named Salvius, and another centurion, Septimius, who had once served under Pompey. These men killed Pompey, on 28

September 48 BC, as he started to rise from the boat to go ashore.

This betrayal of hospitality and former comradeship produced no good results. When Caesar visited Egypt soon afterwards, he turned away with revulsion from the Egyptian who brought him Pompey's head. He burst into tears when Pompey's signet ring was given to him; executed Achillas; and declared war against Ptolemy, eventually deposing him and setting up Cleopatra as monarch. Theodotus escaped, but was found, tortured, and executed by Brutus several years later. The fate of the treacherous Septimius is not recorded. Caesar himself outlived Pompey by less than four years (see p. 21); Plutarch reports that, when he was murdered, he fell down against the pedestal of a statue of Pompey and drenched it with his blood.

Alexander
POPE
(1688–1744)

There is nothing that is meritorious but virtue and friendship; and indeed friendship itself is only a part of virtue.
Joseph Spence,
Anecdotes, Observations, and Characters of Books and Men
(written 1728–44)

Alexander Pope, the master of neo-classical English poetry in the eighteenth century, died in the evening of 30 May 1744 at his riverside villa in Twickenham, where he had lived since 1719.

When Pope referred to 'this long disease, my life' (in *An Epistle to Dr Arbuthnot*), he was speaking both literally and figuratively. A childhood illness, which he blamed on excessive study, left him with a tubercular spine and stunted his growth (at 4ft 6ins tall, he was certainly the shortest of major English poets), and throughout his life he was troubled by headaches and various maladies. His literary career, moreover, was a succession of disputes and bitter quarrels, virulent attacks by and upon him: 'I believe, if any one, early in his life should contemplate the dangerous fate of authors, he would scarce be of their number on any consideration. The life of a Wit is a warfare upon earth', he wrote in 1717. In some respects Pope may well appear to be a petty, malicious, scheming man. Yet his friends – many friendships eventually dissolved in acrimony, but some were lasting and warm – emphasized his kindness and goodness of heart. At the end of his life, at least, Pope apparently achieved serenity, insisting on the security of religious faith and the virtue of friendship.

Pope is principally remembered for his satires and quasi-philosophic poems – exquisitely fashioned, incisively perceptive, although mainly reflecting truisms and trivialities – yet among his less characteristic works are two poems deriving from Hadrian's final verses, which seem to presage Pope's deathbed behaviour. The first of these, a fairly loose rendering which Pope subtitled 'The Heathen to His Departing Soul', is quoted on p. 74. The second, a riposte entitled 'The Dying Christian to His Soul, Ode', refers to 'the pain, the bliss of dying!' and ends with an adaptation of St Paul's words (1 Corinthians 15:55): 'O death, where is thy sting? O grave, where is thy victory?'.

Several of Pope's memorable sayings during his final illness were recorded by the clergyman and author Joseph Spence (1699–1768), who had been his friend for more than a decade. All the following anecotes are derived from this source.

About three weeks before his death, Pope was distributing copies of his *Moral Epistles*. He commented: '**Here am I, like Socrates, distributing my morality among my friends, just as I am dying**'. When Spence agreed with this comparison, Pope added: '**That might be; but you must not expect me now to say any thing like Socrates**'.

On 15 May, after his doctor had told him that his breathing

was easier, his pulse sound, and other prognostics were favourable, Pope said ironically, '**Here am I, dying of a hundred good symptoms!**'.

A short time before his death, Pope stated: '**I am so certain of the soul's being immortal that I seem even to feel it within me, as it were by intuition**'. When asked whether a priest should be called to administer the last rites (Pope was a Roman Catholic), he said: '**I do not suppose that is essential, but it will look right: and I heartily thank you for putting me in mind of it**'.

His last recorded words, spoken on the morning of his death, are those quoted at the head of this entry.

Viscount Bolingbroke (Henry St John) – statesman and philosopher, Pope's friend and patron, inspirer of *An Essay on Man* – was so distressed by the poet's fatal illness that he forgot his meliorist philosophy, which proposed that 'Whatever is, is right'. In his grief he said: 'There is so much trouble in coming into the world and so much meanness in going out of it, that 'tis hardly worth while to be here at all'.

François
RABELAIS
(1494?–1553?)

(a) **Tirez le rideau, la farce est jouée.** [**Bring down the curtain, the farce is over.**]

(b) **Je vais quérir un grand peut-être.** [**I am going to seek a great perhaps.**]

These two famous valedictions which have long been attributed to the French humorist Rabelais appear to be legendary. Their precise source has not been traced, and careful biographers – such as Jean Fleury and Jean Plattard – view them with great suspicion. Every age tends to father its anonymous jokes upon its leading wit, or that of the previous generation: hence the numerous apocryphal witticisms ascribed to Sydney Smith in the early nineteenth century, Oscar Wilde at the turn of the century, and Sir Winston Churchill and Sir Thomas Beecham in the twentieth century. To writers of the sixteenth and seventeenth centuries Rabelais was the epitome of sceptical mockery, so it is not altogether surprising that several sayings of this nature, along with many scandalous anecdotes, have been attributed to him (see also p. 82). A rival tradition, equally unsubstantiated, makes him an exemplary figure for the opposition by claiming that he died as a penitent Catholic. In truth, Rabelais simply disappears from history in 1552 and enters the realm of legend. No authentic account of his death is known, and even its date is uncertain; the traditional date of 9 April 1553 probably has no authority, although it seems that he must have died at some time in 1553 or 1554.

The first of the alleged sayings rests on the commonplace comparison of life to a theatrical performance. Similar deathbed utterances have been attributed to Beethoven (see p. 8) and the Greek philosopher Demonax ('**You may go home, the show is over**'), among others. Sir Walter Raleigh's poem 'What is our life?' is an extended treatment of the same metaphor, imaging life as a 'play of passion' and 'short comedy', and ending:

> The graves that hide us from the searching sun
> Are like drawn curtains when the play is done.
> Thus playing post we to our latest rest,
> Only we die in earnest, that's no jest.

It is, at least, not inappropriate that Rabelais, the great joker and comic philosopher, should be represented as dying after either a wry joke or a sceptical devotion to a quest. Such a quest is described in the last two books of his *Pantagruel*, as the hero and his followers voyage to the Land of Lanterns to consult the infallible Oracle of the Bottle. When the sacred bottle is finally reached, it utters merely the enigmatic word

Rabelais

'Trinc', which apparently signifies 'Drink'; the pronouncement seems to be welcome, but hardly relevant.

Grigori Efimovich
RASPUTIN
(1864?–1916)

Felix, Felix, I'll tell the tsarina.
Alex de Jonge, *The Life and Times of Grigorii Rasputin* (1982)

The mad monk, the man they could not kill, the evil genius of the last era of imperial Russia, the love machine, the debauched charlatan, the holy healer – Rasputin has been called all these things, and even in his lifetime he belonged to the realm of legend where lurid tales are plenty, unquestionable facts are few.

He never was a monk, in the first place; he was a *starets*, or unordained religious man. As a young peasant in Siberia, a carter's son, he was notoriously dissipated, but when he found religion and came to St Petersburg he won increasing fame as a holy man and healer. Not that his dissipation ceased, but he was now able to justify it as a necessary step on the road to salvation. With his piercing gaze, his cryptic utterances, his peasant earthiness and shrewdness, and his almost tangible sexuality, he was irresistible to fashionable society at a time of voguish interest in the occult and of low morals. In November 1905 he was introduced to Tsar Nicholas II and Tsarina Alexandra, and made a favourable impression on Alexandra. When he apparently proved himself able to ease the sufferings of her haemophiliac son, Alexis – even, at times, to effect miraculous cures when the boy was in danger of bleeding to death – he won her complete confidence and devotion.

Time after time, imperial favour saved him from the consequences of his scandalous debauchery, but his growing influence over the governance of Russia was viewed by many with fear or envy. Plots against him were numerous. In 1914 he barely survived an assassination attempt initiated by an unfrocked fanatical monk: stabbed in the stomach by a syphilitic ex-prostitute, Rasputin was severely wounded.

The following year, while Nicholas II was directing his army against a German offensive, Rasputin became chief adviser to the Tsarina and thus the unacknowledged ruler of the country. Affairs, both military and domestic, became increasingly disastrous, and in 1916 another conspiracy was formed. The instigator was Prince Felix Yusupov, a wealthy young nobleman of transvestite tendencies, who recruited four helpers: V. M. Purishkevich, an eccentric extreme right-wing politician; Grand Duke Dimitri Pavlovich, the Tsar's aide; Sukhotin, a young army officer; and a physician named Lazovert. Together – but not very discreetly – they plotted to invite Rasputin to Yusupov's palace in St Petersburg on the night of 16–17 December and to poison him with potassium cyanide.

The plan seemed to succeed, when Rasputin obligingly arrived and consumed poisoned cakes and wine. The problem was that the poison seemed to have no effect on him, apart from making him slightly sleepy. Eventually, unable to stay patient any longer, Yusupov shot him in the chest; Rasputin fell to the ground and seemed to be thoroughly dead. Some minutes later, as Yusupov bent over the body, Rasputin opened his eyes, leapt to his feet, and attacked Yusupov desperately, shouting out '**Felix, Felix**'. Yusupov fled upstairs to his fellow conspirators. Purishkevich ran outside and saw Rasputin hurrying across the courtyard, calling out '**Felix, Felix, I'll tell the tsarina**'. He fired four shots with his revolver, hitting Rasputin twice. For good measure, he kicked the body savagely; later Yusupov, apparently in an erotic frenzy, battered the head with a rubber cosh.

At 5.30 a.m. the conspirators drove to a bridge across the River Neva and threw Rasputin's body into the partially-frozen water, where it was found by police on the next day. Some accounts say that an autopsy showed traces of water in the lungs, suggesting that Rasputin was still alive when he entered the river; some claim even that he had burst the bonds tying his hands. These may, however, be merely further strands in the legend of Rasputin's superhuman strength which seemingly enabled him to withstand poisons and bullets.

The assassins were easily traced and put under house arrest. But the mills of justice, while beginning to grind slowly, were overtaken by the revolution in February 1917 which led to the deposition and murder of the royal family. No further action was taken against the murderers, who were free to meet their various fates: Purishkevich to die of typhus while fighting with the White Army in civil war against the new régime, and Yusupov to live on in exile for many years. The murder of Rasputin had no direct link with the revolution, but it was rather more than a symptom of something rotten in the state. The killers, who had wanted to save the old system by removing the corrupting influence of Rasputin, had in fact dealt a fatal blow to the authority of imperial rule.

Cecil
RHODES
(1853–1902)

On the afternoon of Wednesday, the 26th March, I sat for a while by his bedside, while Dr Jameson, worn out by persistent watching day and night, took a short rest. The patient was restless and uneasy. Once he murmured, '**So little done, so much to do**', and then after a long pause I heard him singing softly to himself, maybe a few bars of an air he had once sung at his mother's knee. Then, in a clear voice, he called for Jameson. I slipped away to my own house a few miles off, intending to return later in the evening, but within an hour came the fatal telegram that, to the accompaniment of the thunder of the surf breaking on the beach in front of his little bedroom, the greatest of modern Englishmen had passed away.

Sir Lewis Michell,
The Life of the Rt. Hon. Cecil John Rhodes (1910)

Cecil Rhodes died peacefully on 26 March 1902, shortly before the end of the Boer War, in his house at Muizenberg, near Cape Town. The last word he uttered was the name of Dr Jameson (Sir Leander Starr Jameson), his associate whose ill-fated raid into the Transvaal in 1896, designed to overthrow Paul Kruger's anti-British government, had led to Rhodes's resignation as Prime Minister of the Cape Colony and precipitated the Boer War. Rhodes's last full statement, quoted above, is actually an adaptation of lines from section LXXIII of Tennyson's *In Memoriam*:

So many worlds, so much to do,
So little done, such things to be.

Rhodes's principles and achievements, which had many detractors even in his own time, have become as unfashionable as the hyperbolic style of his biographer. The fifth son of a clergyman in Bishop's Stortford, he was first sent to Southern Africa – in 1870 – for the sake of his health. Having amassed a fortune in diamonds, he returned to Britain a couple of years later; but in 1873 he went back to Africa after a further breakdown of health which was so serious that, although Rhodes did not know it at the time, his doctor gave him less than six months to live. So, more or less accidentally, began the career which led to his becoming Prime Minister of the Cape Colony and managing director of the British South Africa Company, procuring much of the territory of Bechuana and Matabele for the British empire, and developing the new country of Rhodesia (now Zambia and Zimbabwe).

Memorials of the imperialist Rhodes are now being eradicated in Africa, while his own countrymen profess themselves embarrassed by his belief that Britain had the right and duty to govern the world.

Armand-Jean du Plessis de
RICHELIEU
(1585–1642)

My niece, there are no truths except those in the gospel; it is in them alone that one should believe.
Gabriel Hanotaux and Le Duc de La Force,
Histoire du Cardinal de Richelieu, Vol. VI (1947);
D. P. O'Connell, *Richelieu* (1968)

On 2 and 3 December 1642 King Louis XIII of France came to visit his chief minister, on hearing that Cardinal Richelieu's illness (diagnosed as pleurisy) was likely to prove fatal. From his deathbed Richelieu reaffirmed his devotion to his country and religion, and the two men made their farewells. Thus ended an improbable but effective working relationship, lasting for eighteen years and creating a powerful Catholic France, between partners of contrasting temperaments. While intensely disliking Richelieu personally, the King recognized – and became dependent on – his invaluable political talents. Richelieu, in turn, cannot have found the monarch a person to be loved or greatly respected: a tubercular, neurasthenic, chronically hypochondriac, despotic, and ultimately weak man.

Richelieu had long been aware, in addition, that royal favour was capricious. Keeping his own position secure against conspiracies was an art in which he mercilessly excelled. The King's brother, Gaston of Orleans, had once plotted unsuccessfully against him. Then the Queen Mother, Marie de Médicis, had very nearly gained the dismissal of her former adviser by violently denouncing him to her son. Richelieu's last months had been clouded by a conspiracy against him by Henri d'Effiat, the Marquis de Cinq Mars, an aristocratic libertine, once Richelieu's protégé, who had become a royal favourite and quarrelled with Richelieu. At this time, too, the red-robed eminence had lost the services of his confidant and adviser, Père Joseph (died in 1638), a Capuchin friar who combined mysticism with slippery diplomacy and was nicknamed the Grey Eminence on account of the colour of his habit. But, with the help of his immense intelligence network, Richelieu was able to forestall Cinq Mars and ensure that the young man was executed.

Such was the fate of the enemies of Richelieu, who – although no hypocrite or self-seeker – appreciated the value of ruthlessness as well as the comforts of religion. He could afford to be more tolerant in his last moments. At midday on 4 December he summoned his niece, the Duchesse d'Aiguillon, to his official residence, the Palais Cardinal. He told her that he loved and respected her more than anyone else and that she must therefore leave him, since it would not be appropriate for her to see him expire. She replied encouragingly that she had been told of a vision that he would not die of this illness. He then spoke the words above, asserting that the only truths are those of the gospel, and implicitly rejecting the secular world of power politics. She left him, and he died peacefully a little later.

Marie-Jeanne
ROLAND
(1754–1793)

> Ô Liberté! que de crimes on commet en ton nom!
> [O Liberty! what crimes are committed in your name!]
> Gita May, *Madame Roland and the Age of Revolution* (1970)

Marie-Jeanne (familiarly called Manon) Phlipon, an engraver's daughter, was a studious and high-minded girl with an optimistic view of human nature and a firm belief in the dignity of the individual. In 1780 she married Jean-Marie Roland de la Platière, an inspector of manufactures, and after moving to Paris the couple became prominent among the Girondists, the moderate faction of revolutionaries. Although the man had to be the public figure – he became Minister of the Interior in March 1792 – there is no doubt that Mme Roland wrote his letters and speeches, directed his activities, and was, for a short time, virtual ruler of France. But Roland was forced to resign in January 1793, as a consequence of the bitter rivalry between the Girondists and the more radical Jacobins, who included such men as Maximilien Robespierre and Georges Jacques Danton; and at the end of May the Jacobin faction purged the Girondists.

Jean-Marie Roland managed to escape to Rouen, but his wife was arrested. After five months in prison – a time she spent in writing her memoirs – she was brought to trial before the Revolutionary Tribunal on 8 November. The proceedings were brief and scarcely impartial; she was convicted of conspiracy against the Republic, and sentenced to be executed on the same day. She ate a final lunch, had her long brown hair shorn, and – in the company of an elderly forger named Lamarche – was taken in the tumbril to the guillotine set up in the Place de la Révolution. Her behaviour, all eyewitnesses agree, was totally calm and dignified; the only sign of any emotion was an enigmatic smile flickering on her lips.

Before mounting the ladder to the platform on the guillotine, she looked at the huge clay statue of Liberty which had been erected in the square, and uttered the famous phrase quoted above.

Three days later the body of her husband was found by a roadside near Rouen. He had stabbed himself three times with a sword-stick, leaving two messages in his pocket. In one he begged to be remembered as a man '**who died as he had lived, in honesty and virtue**'; in the other he explained that his motive was not fear but indignation: '**I left my refuge as soon as I learned my wife was murdered; I no longer wished to remain on an earth covered with such crimes**'.

The fates of their rivals and enemies were scarcely happier. Jean-Paul Marat, the radical journalist who frequently attacked them, had been assassinated in his bath by Charlotte Corday on 15 July 1793, immediately after uttering a bloody threat against the Girondists who had fled to Caen: '**Before eight days have passed, they will all have gone to the guillotine**'. Danton, overthrown by Robespierre, was guillotined on 5 April 1794: reputedly his last words, addressed to the executioner, were: '**You will show my head to the people. 'Tis worth looking at**'. Robespierre, overthrown in turn by a coup d'état, lost his head on 28 July 1794.

Nicola SACCO
(1891–1927)

and

Bartolomeo VANZETTI
(1888–1927)

SACCO **Long live anarchy! – Farewell my wife and child and all my friends. – Good evening, gentlemen. – Farewell! – Mother!**

VANZETTI **I wish to say to you that I am innocent. I have never done a crime, some sins, but never any crime. I thank you for everything you have done for me. I am innocent of all crime, not only this one, but of all, of all. I am an innocent man. – I now wish to forgive some people for what they are doing to me.**

Francis Russell, Tragedy in Dedham (1963)

The 'Sacco-Vanzetti case' was a long-running sensation, not only in the United States but elsewhere, and it remains an issue to which people react not with objective judgment but with an instant emotional or political bias. Two poor left-wing Italian immigrants, executed for murder: were they reckless criminals, misguided idealists, or innocent victims of political and racial prejudice?

Both men had emigrated in 1908 to the United States, where Sacco worked in a shoe factory while Vanzetti peddled fish from a barrow. Both were revolutionary anarchists, involved in a group in New England which distributed propaganda and was popularly considered responsible for various terrorist activities. Accused of murdering a guard and a paymaster during a payroll robbery at South Braintree, Massachusetts, in 1921 they were tried and convicted of first-degree murder. The evidence against them was circumstantial and sometimes conflicting, and the trial took place against a background of Red scares and hostility against immigrants. Their conviction caused an outcry in several quarters, and was followed by years of appeal and controversy. In 1925 a convicted criminal named Celestino Madeiros confessed that he had been one of a gang which committed the murders, but his evidence was not entirely satisfactory. In 1927 Sacco and Vanzetti were condemned to death, but protests and appeals from many parts of the world led to a stay of execution. A special independent committee set up by the governor of Massachusetts now reviewed the case, but came to the conclusion that the trial had been fair. The two men were electrocuted, together with Madeiros, at Charlestown prison, Boston, on 23 August 1927. In their last moments Sacco was defiant, Vanzetti calmly proclaimed his innocence.

At the time of their arrest, both men spoke little English. During their years in prison they improved their knowledge of the language, but never fully mastered it; and one cannot help wondering whether their linguistic vulnerability has not contributed greatly to the image of them as victims. Their colourful broken English gives their later writings and speeches a poignant quality; one tends to disbelieve that men using language with such childlike innocence, or such evocative poetic force, could really be violent criminals. Vanzetti describes the flowers in his cell: 'My window here is peopled of recipients, it is a riot of blissing colors and beauties forms: a giranium plants a tulipan plant from Mrs Evans'. He predicts a time when knowledge of the case will be 'a deem rememoring of a cursed past in which man was wolf to the man'. He announces his determination 'to rivendicate our right to live and be free, but all the forces of the State and of the Money and reaction are deadly against us because we are libertarian or anarchist'.

Is this the language of a murderer? It could be; for it is certainly the language of an outcast from the world of respectable prose, whether he is a foreigner, a poet, or a criminal. The truth of the case cannot now be ascertained. They may both have been guilty; they may both have been innocent; or, as Francis Russell argues persuasively, Sacco was guilty while Vanzetti, although innocent, refused to save himself by betraying his comrade.

SAMSON

And Samson called unto the Lord, and said, '**O Lord God, remember me, I pray thee, and strengthen me, I pray thee, only this once, O God, that I may be at once avenged of the Philistines for my two eyes**'.
And Samson took hold of the two middle pillars upon which the house stood, and on which it was borne up, of the one with his right hand, and of the other with his left.
And Samson said, '**Let me die with the Philistines**'. And he bowed himself with all his might; and the house fell upon the lords, and upon all the people that were therein.
Judges 16:28–30

Samson, the Israelite hero who repeatedly smote the Philistines hip and thigh yet had an insuperable predilection for Philistine women, finally revealed to Delilah the secret of his enormous strength: it lay in his hair, which, in accordance with his consecration as a Nazarite at birth, had never been cut. Delilah betrayed him to the Philistines; they shaved his head, blinded him, and set him to work grinding corn in the prison at Gaza. Some time later, at a great festival in honour of their god Dagon, his enemies brought him into the temple to mock him. Samson, whose hair had grown again, with a final show of strength demolished the building, killing more than three thousand people with himself.

The story of Samson, as presented in the Bible, contains many elements which resemble folk-tales or have analogues in other mythologies. Although there may be a core of historical reality in this account of his exploits, many scholars now consider him a legendary figure, perhaps intended to point the moral of the dangers of breaking one's vows or consorting with strange women.

SAUL
(died *ca* 1000 BC)

(a) Then said Saul unto his armour-bearer, '**Draw thy sword, and thrust me through therewith; lest these uncircumcised come and thrust me through, and abuse me**'. But his armour-bearer would not; for he was sore afraid. Therefore Saul took a sword, and fell upon it.
1 Samuel 31:4

(b) He said unto me again, '**Stand, I pray thee, upon me, and slay me: for anguish is come upon me, because my life is yet whole in me**'.
So I stood upon him, and slew him, because I was sure that he could not live after that he was fallen.
2 Samuel 1:9–10

Saul, son of Kish, of the tribe of Benjamin, became the first king of Israel about 1020 BC. According to the biblical account in 1 Samuel, the Israelites – previously ruled by a judge – insisted upon having a monarchy in imitation of other nations; whereupon Saul, the tallest man in Israel, was elected as king through the favour of Samuel, the last judge, who later repented supporting him.

Under Saul's leadership, the Israelites fought and defeated the Amalekites, Ammonites, and Philistines. His reign was dominated, however, by his relationship with David – originally his protégé and son-in-law, and the close friend of his eldest and favourite son Jonathan, but later his deadly rival. Fearful and confused when the Philistine forces reassembled for battle with David on their side, Saul consulted the Witch of Endor, 'a woman that hath a familiar spirit'. She conjured up the ghost of Samuel, whose message was scarcely encouraging: he foretold that Saul's disobedience to the voice of the Lord would lead to his defeat and death, and the passing of his crown to David.

David did not, after all, take part in the subsequent battle at Mount Gilboa. But there Saul was killed, together with his three sons – Jonathan, Abinadab, and Melchi-shua – and the Israelites were routed.

Three separate accounts of Saul's death are offered in the Bible. The narrative in 1 Chronicles 10 is almost identical to the one in 1 Samuel, and is clearly based either on that or on the same source. The discrepant versions in 1 and 2 Samuel doubtless stem from the nature of those two books: both are patchworks of summaries and extracts from divers sources, edited by various hands at various times, and probably also changed by copyists. It is therefore impossible to decide which of them should be credited.

According to 1 Samuel, at Gilboa Saul was 'sore wounded of the archers' and killed himself (see (a) above). It is perhaps suspicious that a rather similar end is recorded of Abimelech, one of Gideon's seventy sons, who, after having all but one of his brothers killed, tried to establish a monarchy. While storming the rebellious city of Thebez, he had his skull broken by a piece of millstone thrown down at him by a woman in a tower. He then instructed his armour-bearer: **'Draw thy sword, and slay me, that men say not of me, A woman slew him**' (Judges 9:53–54).

2 Samuel, however, tells of David returning from his separate and successful battle against the Amalekites and finding a young man 'with his clothes rent, and earth upon his head'. This man, an Amalekite, told him of the disaster at Gilboa and related that he himself, coming by chance across the wounded Saul, had been persuaded to dispatch him (see (b) above). It is not clear whether the Amalekite's story was a reluctant confession, or (as David implies in 2 Samuel 4:10) a boast intended to bring him rewards. In either case he was

unfortunate, for at once David had him put to death and then uttered his famous lament over Saul and Jonathan with the refrain 'How are the mighty fallen!'

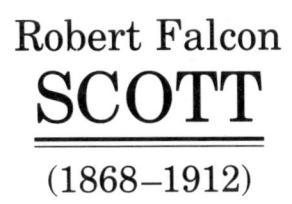

Robert Falcon
SCOTT
(1868–1912)

For God's sake look after our people.
last entry in his *Journal*, 29 March 1912

After the departure of Lawrence Oates (see p. 126), the Antarctic expedition led by Scott – a naval officer who had commanded an earlier Antarctic voyage in 1901–4 – struggled on for a few more days until an impassable blizzard confined the three survivors in a tent, with their supplies almost exhausted. Although knowing that they were only eleven miles from a depot, in the conditions they were unable to move at all. 'I do not think we can hope for any better things now', Scott wrote. 'We shall stick it out to the end, but we are getting weaker, of course, and the end cannot be far'.

Search parties sent to relieve them were driven back by the weather. Not until November 1912 was the tent found, with the bodies of the three men. It appeared that Scott had died after his colleagues; his arm was round Wilson, and under his shoulder were the notebooks in which he had recorded events almost until the end.

Scott's final wish was fulfilled. After the news of the disaster reached Britain, a successful fund was set up to provide for the relatives of the dead explorers. Scott's widow, Kathleen – a noted sculptress – was granted by royal warrant the rank and precedence of the wife of a KCB; his son, Sir Peter Scott (born in 1909), later achieved fame as an artist and ornithologist.

SOCRATES
(470?–399 BC)

He walked about until, as he said, his legs began to fail, and then he lay on his back, according to the directions, and the man who gave him the poison now and then looked at his feet and legs; and after a while he pressed his foot hard, and asked him if he could feel; and he said, '**No**'; and then his leg, and so upwards and upwards, and showed us that he was cold and stiff. And he felt them himself, and said: '**When the poison reaches the heart, that will be the end**'. He was beginning to grow cold about the groin, when he uncovered his face, for he had covered himself up, and said – they were his last words – '**Crito, I owe a cock to Asclepius; will you remember to pay the debt?**' The debt shall be paid, said Crito; is there anything else? There was no answer to this question; but in a minute or two a movement was heard, and the attendants uncovered him; his eyes were set, and Crito closed his eyes and mouth.

Plato, *Phaedo* (translated by Benjamin Jowett)

In 399 BC the Athenian philosopher Socrates was indicted on two counts of impiety: of 'denying the gods recognized by the state and introducing new divinities', and of 'corrupting the young'. At his trial, instead of denying the charges he merely treated them with contempt. By a majority verdict he was found guilty and sentenced to death. This sentence could almost certainly have been commuted, had Socrates proposed an alternative punishment (i.e. a fine); but, insisting on the contrary that he deserved not punishment but reward, Socrates so exasperated the judges that the death penalty was confirmed.

It was the practice for a condemned man to drink poison

made from the hemlock plant. Normally death took place on the day after the trial; but, because of a rule that no one should be put to death during the annual voyage of a sacred ship to Delos, Socrates had to wait in prison for thirty days. During that time (described in Plato's *Crito*) he conversed with his friends, arguing that death should be approached cheerfully and confidently, and rejected an escape plan made by his friend Crito.

Socrates' death was described in detail by his disciple Plato (*ca* 427–347 BC), who, although not an eye-witness of the event, was in close touch with many witnesses. Plato tells of Socrates drinking the cup of poison 'quite readily and cheerfully', then rebuking his companions for weeping: '**A man should die in peace**', he said.

Socrates' last words allude to the custom of offering a sacrifice (such as a cock) to Asclepius (or Aesculapius), the Greek god of medicine, after one was healed. Their purport, however, is debatable. Several commentators have suggested that Socrates was implying that human life itself was a sickness of which death would heal him. But this interpretation, tempting as it is, does not accord with the views on life which Socrates expressed elsewhere. It is more probable that, quite simply, in his last moments Socrates remembered an unfulfilled vow which he had made on some earlier occasion.

When Plato himself was at the point of death he gave thanks to fortune and his guardian spirit '**first, that he was born a man and a Greek, not a barbarian nor an irrational animal; and then, that he was born in the time when Socrates lived**' (Plutarch, *Life of Gaius Marius*). Socrates' death has exercised a powerful influence on later generations. The Roman statesman Cato the Younger read *Phaedo* the night before he killed himself. Joseph Addison (see p. 1) represented this in his play *Cato*. Eustace Budgell (see p. 19) had Cato and Addison on his mind. Alexander Pope (see p. 142), on his deathbed, self-deprecatingly compared himself to Socrates.

Gertrude
STEIN
(1874–1946)

(a) I sat next to her and she said to me early in the afternoon, **'What is the answer?** I was silent. **'In that case,**' she said, **'what is the question?'**

    Alice B. Toklas, *What Is Remembered* (1963)

(b) About Baby's last words. She said upon waking from a sleep **'What is the question'**. And I didnt answer thinking she was not completely awakened. Then she said again – **'What is the question'** and before I could speak she went on – **'If there is no question then there is no answer'**. And she turned and went to sleep again.

    Alice B. Toklas, letter to Carl Van Vechten, 24 April 1953, in *Staying On Alone: Letters of Alice B. Toklas* (1974)

Gertrude Stein died on 27 July 1946 in the American hospital at Neuilly in France, never recovering consciousness after a desperate operation on a far-advanced cancer. Her last words were spoken – just before she was taken to the operating theatre – to her companion Alice B. Toklas, with whom she had lived in Paris since 1907, and whose purported autobiography (*The Autobiography of Alice B. Toklas*) she had written. Unfortunately Toklas herself has posed a question to which there is no answer, by giving two rather different accounts of Stein's last words. Version (a) is the well-known one – and apparently the earlier, since Donald Sutherland relates it in his *Gertrude Stein: A Biography of her Work* (1951). But why did Toklas tell a different story in 1953: was she temporarily forgetful, or confusing legend with reality?

Of one point there can be no doubt: this fundamental self-questioning was a most appropriate final utterance. Toklas calls Stein's words 'a summing up of her life'; Sutherland comments that 'they say what she had always been saying'.

After a conventional upbringing in the United States, Stein had emigrated to Europe in 1920 and devoted herself to the sceptical, questioning spirit in modern art and literature. It was she who popularized the phrase 'the lost generation', referring to the young people of the 1920s; she who championed such artists as Picasso, Braque, and Matisse, and befriended Ernest Hemingway, Scott Fitzgerald, and other writers. Her own experimental writing, difficult and frequently tiresome as it is, may be seen as a bold attempt to pose fundamental – and probably unanswerable – queries and paradoxes in the simplest language, as in her much-parodied phrase 'rose is a rose is a rose'. An eccentric and rather terrifying *grande dame*, to many of her contemporaries she was a strange object to be approached with a mixture of awe, gratitude, and mockery; the American writer Clifford Fadiman memorably dubbed her 'the mama of dada'. Later writers may scorn her sexual tastes and her deficient understanding of the artists and writers she tried to help; still, a brave, independent woman, she remains a significant figure of intellectual life between the wars.

Saint
STEPHEN
(died *ca* 36)

Lord, lay not this sin to their charge.
Acts 7:60

St Stephen, the first Christian martyr, was one of the 'seven men of honest report' chosen to administer the finance and alms of the early Church in Jerusalem. He was known as 'a man full of faith and of the Holy Ghost' who 'did great wonders and miracles among the people' (Acts 6:5, 8). The nature of these wonders and miracles must remain uncertain,

Stephen

for our single source of information about Stephen is this brief biblical account.

He was apprehended and brought before the Sanhedrin (the supreme rabbinic court in Jerusalem) on charges of speaking blasphemously, saying that Jesus would destroy the Temple and change the old dispensation. In his defence he denounced the Jews for resisting divine guidance, persecuting the prophets, and murdering Jesus; he then looked upwards and asserted that he was receiving a divine vision. In fury his accusers 'cast him out of the city, and stoned him'. Stephen cried out '**Lord Jesus, receive my spirit**' – a cry which has been echoed by several later martyrs (for example, Hugh Latimer (see p. 99), John Hooper, and Rowland Taylor, all burnt in 1555). He then knelt down and, just before dying, spoke the words quoted above.

One of the eye-witnesses of his death was a young Jew named Saul, who distinguished himself by his zeal in furthering the subsequent persecution of Christians. 'And when the blood of thy martyr Stephen was shed, I also was standing by, and consenting unto his death, and kept the raiment of them that slew him', he declared later (Acts 22:1) – by which time, following his conversion on the road to Damascus, he had taken the name of Paul and become one of the foremost apostles.

Laurence STERNE
(1713–1768)

I went to Mr Sterne's lodging; the mistress opened the door; I inquired how he did. She told me to go up to the nurse. I went into the room, and he was just a-dying. I waited ten minutes; but in five he said: '**Now it is come**'. He put up his hand as if to stop a blow, and died in a minute.

John Macdonald,
Travels in Various Parts of Europe, Asia, and Africa (1790)

The author of this narrative——ye heavens! men and angels might blub at the perusing of it——must be pricked out *suo jure* as a man beyond the ordinary——A footman he was——nay, he need not blush to admit it, for merit subsisteth in the *vivendi*, not in the *operandi*——acquainted with great men——honoured with the sobriquet of Beau——who travelled to divers parts with his masters——of which ventures he hath written a volume to be commended to the generous spirits of all nations——

Who can resist the unique style of Laurence Sterne? A manner of writing that is also a mode of thinking; a superficial imitation may be easy enough, but the cast of Sterne's mind is inimitable. It must have taken shape in obscurity and wry despair during almost twenty relatively uneventful years as a clergyman in Yorkshire before he was catapulted into fame or notoriety in 1760 by the publication of the first two volumes of his eccentric comic masterpiece, *Tristram Shandy*. For a time he was the lion of literary society, until illness forced him to go abroad in January 1762 for the sake of his health. This journey is clearly reflected in Volume VII of *Tristram Shandy*, which includes many heterodox meditations on illness and death prefiguring the manner of his dying. In Chapter 12, for instance, Sterne specifies how he wishes to die:

> Was I in a condition to stipulate with Death... I should certainly declare against submitting to it before my friends; and therefore, I never seriously think upon the mode and manner of this great catastrophe, which generally takes up and torments my thoughts as much as the catastrophe itself, but I constantly draw the curtain across it with this wish, that the Disposer of all things may so order it, that it happen not to me in my own house——but rather in some decent inn——at home, I know it,——the concern of my friends, and the last services of wiping my brows and soothing my pillow, which the quivering hand of pale

affection shall pay me, will so crucify my soul that I shall die of a distemper which my physician is not aware of: but in an inn, the few cold offices I wanted would be purchased with a few guineas, and paid me with an undisturbed but punctual attention——

Sterne died of pleurisy on 18 March 1768 (just a few weeks after publication of his *A Sentimental Journey through France and Italy*), in lodgings at 41 Old Bond Street, London; away from his home in Coxwold, his estranged wife, his daughter, and his mistress, perhaps in the manner he wished – certainly, if Macdonald's account is true, in a calm and dignified way. Yet fate may have kept in reserve a few more bizarre indignities to heap upon him; for there were widespread rumours after his death that his corpse, buried in St George's cemetery in Bayswater Road, was disinterred by body-snatchers and sold to Charles Collignon, professor of anatomy at Cambridge. In 1968 the Laurence Sterne Trust excavated the supposed site of Sterne's grave, and uncovered a skull and other bones which they believed to be his. The top of the skull had been sawn off, as if by a surgical instrument; a possible explanation is that Sterne did indeed fall into the hands of anatomists who, belatedly recognizing that the body was that of a famous man, secretly returned the mutilated remains.

Italo
SVEVO
(1861–1928)

(a) **That really would have been the last cigarette.**

(b) **When you haven't prayed all your life, it's no use at the last moment.**
Livia Veneziani Svevo, *Vita di mio marito* (1976),
and P. N. Furbank, *Italo Svevo: The Man and the Writer* (1966)

Italo Svevo ('Italian Swabian') was the pseudonym of Ettore Schmitz, a Jewish native of Trieste who is gradually gaining recognition as one of the subtlest and most astringent of modern novelists.

Discouraged by the reception given to his first two novels, for several years Svevo abandoned his literary ambitions and concentrated on his work as manager of a company making anti-corrosive paint for ships' hulls. For the purpose of business contacts he needed to improve his English, and in 1907 began taking lessons from a young expatriate Irishman. That was the turning point in his life; for the teacher was James Joyce, who appreciated Svevo's real talents and encouraged him to resume writing. The result was his masterpiece, *The Confessions of Zeno*, published in 1924, a subtle ironic comedy of which one of the chief themes is a man's desperate attempts to give up smoking – or, rather, on his devious ploys to postpone giving up smoking and his frequent excuses for smoking 'one last cigarette'.

On 12 September 1928, Svevo was returning with his wife and grandson from a holiday in the Italian Alps. Crossing a bridge at Vecchia Collalta, near Motta di Livenza, their chauffeur-driven car skidded and hit a tree. Although Svevo's injuries were not very serious, the shock brought on heart failure, and he died in hospital the next morning.

On his deathbed he saw his daughter Letizia crying, and said to her: '**Don't cry, Letizia; dying is nothing**'. A nurse asked his wife if a priest should be summoned to administer the last rites; she hesitated and asked Svevo, who commented on the futility of a deathbed conversion (see (b) above). Seeing his nephew smoking, Svevo made a gesture that he too wanted a cigarette; when this was refused him, he made a sardonic reference to the theme of *Zeno* and his own addiction to tobacco (see (a) above). His biographers disagree about the order in which these last two statements were made; Furbank places (a) after (b), but his widow states that (b) was his last utterance.

Zenzaburo TAKI
(1835?–1868)

After another profound obeisance, Taki Zenzaburo, in a voice which betrayed just so much emotion and hesitation as might be expected from a man who is making a painful confession, but with no sign of either in his face or manner, spoke as follows:-
'**I, and I alone, unwarrantably gave the order to fire on the foreigners at Kobe, and again as they tried to escape. For this crime I disembowel myself, and I beg you who are present to do me the honour of witnessing the act.**'
Bowing once more, the speaker allowed his upper garments to slip down to his girdle, and remained naked to the waist. Carefully, according to custom, he tucked his sleeves under his knees to prevent himself from falling backwards; for a noble Japanese gentleman should die falling forwards. Deliberately, with a steady hand, he took the dirk that lay before him; he looked at it wistfully, almost affectionately; for a moment he seemed to collect his thoughts for the last time, and then stabbing himself deeply below the waist on the left-hand side, he drew the dirk

slowly across to the right side, and, turning it in the wound, gave a slight cut upwards. During this sickeningly painful operation he never moved a muscle of his face. When he drew out the dirk, he leaned forward and stretched out his neck; an expression of pain for the first time crossed his face, but he uttered no sound. At that moment the *kaishaku*, who, still crouching by his side, had been keenly watching his every movement, sprang to his feet, poised his sword for a second in the air; there was a flash, a heavy, ugly thud, a crashing fall; with one blow the head had been severed from the body.

A dead silence followed, broken only by the hideous noise of the blood throbbing out of the inert heap before us, which but a moment before had been a brave and chivalrous man. It was horrible.

A. B. Mitford, *Tales of Old Japan* (1871)

This remarkable detailed narrative is the earliest known eye-witness account by a westerner of the Japanese practice of suicide by ritual self-disembowelment. This ancient custom is generally known in the West as *hara-kiri* (literally meaning 'belly cutting'), but in Japan itself it is always called *seppuku*. Traditionally it was restricted to members of the samurai (military class), and could be either voluntary or compulsory. Voluntary seppuku might be performed to save oneself from the disgrace of surrendering to an enemy, out of desperation, or as an act of protest. Compulsory seppuku was, in effect, a means of capital punishment intended to allow the guilty man to maintain honour and dignity by killing himself rather than sharing the fate of common criminals who were beheaded. The prescribed ritual in such cases became particularly complex, involving the construction of a special site, the wearing of ceremonial dress, elaborate formality, and a confession of guilt. In many instances, the disembowelment was partly or wholly symbolic – the victim might wound himself only superficially, or might merely lean forward to pick up a dagger – and was not in itself the cause of death. The coup de grâce was administered by a second, known as a *kaishaku* and nearly always a relative, friend, or pupil of the victim, who beheaded the man with a razor-sharp sword.

For over 200 years the Japanese policy of isolation kept the country almost entirely cut off from the rest of the world. Not until the second half of the nineteenth century were foreigners allowed into Japan, and even then they were distrusted, restricted, and sometimes endangered. On 11 January 1868, in the port of Kobe, where the foreign legations had taken refuge from the civil war being fought in parts of the country, a group of Japanese soldiers – considering themselves grossly insulted by a breach of etiquette when two Westerners crossed the road ahead of them – suddenly opened fire. Although only two or three minor casualties ensued before guards from the legations chased the soldiers away, serious international repercussions seemed imminent. The Japanese officer who had given the order to fire was therefore held responsible, and was instructed by the Mikado (Emperor) to put an end to his life in accordance with tradition. The ceremony was performed in the temple of Eifukuji at Hyogo at 10.30 p.m. on 9 February 1868. Seven foreign witnesses – one from each of the resident legations – were invited to attend; among them was A. B. (Freeman-) Mitford, then second secretary to the British legation.

Compulsory seppuku was prevalent from the fifteenth century until 1873, when it was abolished. Voluntary seppuku, however, is still occasionally practised; the most famous recent case was that of the novelist Yukio Mishima, who disembowelled himself publicly in Tokyo on 25 November 1970 as a protest against the decadence and demilitarization of modern Japan.

Henry David
THOREAU
(1817–1862)

> The last sentence he incompletely spoke contained but two
> distinct words, '**moose**' and '**Indian**'.
> William Ellery Channing, *Thoreau, the Poet-Naturalist* (1873)

Thoreau, now recognized as one of the most original and perceptive of nineteenth-century American writers, died of tuberculosis on 6 May 1862 at Concord, Massachusetts. In or near that small, respectable, microcosmic (and, from Thoreau's point of view, none too aptly named) town he had spent nearly all his life, despite writing of it that 'every where, in shops, and offices, and fields, the inhabitants have appeared to me to be doing penance in a thousand remarkable ways'.

He was a nonconformist: not a revolutionary, but a stubborn, unpredictable individualist. He rejected the orthodox; he sought the paradox. 'The mass of men lead lives of quiet desperation', he proclaimed; and 'Most of the luxuries, and many of the so called comforts of life, are not only not indispensable, but positive hinderances to the elevation of mankind'. In an attempt to reduce his life to essentials, for over two years Thoreau lived in a homemade cabin in the woods outside Concord. This experiment – described in his masterpiece, *Walden* – was not prompted wholly by escapism or naive idealism; he viewed it as a practical demonstration of how easily a man can live well, and as his declaration of independence from a repressive society. Having made his point, he returned to the penitential life of the town.

Thoreau's barely articulate last words – uttered between eight and nine o'clock on a beautiful spring morning, and recorded by his most intimate friend, the eccentric poet Ellery Channing – united two of his preoccupations: wildlife and the American Indian. These were not fashionable subjects in Thoreau's lifetime. The good people of Concord laughed scornfully at a man who spent hours observing a frog – or, remembering how his carelessness had resulted in the burning of three hundred acres of woodland, they were scarcely eager to listen when he lectured them on the importance of the natural environment. Nor could they look except with scorn, fear, or pity upon the American Indians, in whom Thoreau had been passionately interested since his childhood, and whom he saw as a link between nature and civilized man. By reading, searching for relics, and interviewing Indians, he collected a mass of materials for a projected book upon the subject.

Possibly a more specific connection between 'moose' and 'Indian' may be traced. In 1853 Thoreau had gone on an expedition into the woods of Maine with his cousin George Thatcher and an Indian guide. Thoreau was keen to see a moose; his cousin was keen to shoot one, and succeeded. Thoreau was greatly distressed by this wanton killing, and particularly by the sight of the Indian skinning the still-warm carcase. Perhaps a memory of this traumatic event – a reminder of death and human cruelty, an evocation of guilt and helplessness – haunted him in his last moments.

Thoreau's last illness was long, and several of his sayings during this time have been falsely described as his last words. In the spring of 1862 he said to a friend '**I shall leave the world without regret**'; only a little while before, he had written '**I am enjoying existence as much as ever, and regret nothing**'. About the beginning of May, when his aunt asked him if he had made his peace with God, he replied '**I did not know we had ever quarrelled**' – see p. 77 for Heine's reply to the same question. (Thoreau also said that 'a snow-storm was more to him than Christ'. By refusing to pay his church tax bill in 1846, he had effectively announced his resignation from the Christian church. He was certainly a man of religious spirit, but organized religion was anathema to him; pantheism and Buddhism were more to his taste.) Other recorded utterances include: '**It is better some things should end**'; '**This is a beautiful world, but I shall see a fairer'; and 'When I was a very little boy I learned that I must die, and I set that down, so of course I am not disappointed now'. Details may be found in Walter Harding's fine biography, *The Days of Henry Thoreau* (revised edition, 1982).

James
THURBER
(1894–1961)

God bless... God damn.
Burton Bernstein, *Thurber: A Biography* (1975)

Thurber's last recorded words, a blessing and a curse, may present a particularly apt summary of his mixed feelings and fortunes. He was a humorist, but a man subject to severe depressions. His writings and cartoons, which to some seemed whimsical and purely comic, were always wry, sometimes deeply melancholy. His recurrent subject was the confusion and alienation of modern man; the humorous treatment does not dissolve the seriousness of the theme but often serves to emphasize it. Even the titles of some of his later works exemplify the two sides of his work and character: *Alarms and Diversions, Lanterns and Lances, Credos and Curios*. His many successes were blended, increasingly, with disappointments and failures. His sight, on which he depended, failed; at the age of six he was blinded in the left eye by a toy arrow shot by one of his brothers, and the other eye deteriorated to leave him totally blind by the end of the 1940s. Illness and disenchantment with the state of the world made him an increasingly bitter and estranged man in his later years; 'Nowadays most men lead lives of noisy desperation' he wrote, parodying Thoreau (see p. 171), in *Further Fables for Our Time*.

Thurber

Thurber was taken to Doctors Hospital in New York City on 4 October 1961, following his collapse on the morning after a party at which he had behaved exceptionally erratically, and on the day of his admission an emergency operation was performed to remove a blood tumour on his brain. For nearly four weeks he remained virtually comatose, partially paralysed. His daughter, Rosemary, once heard him mutter '**God ... God ... God**'; his wife, Helen Muriel Wismer, heard him whisper the words quoted above. Thurber then developed pneumonia and fell into a deep coma. His end came suddenly on the afternoon of 2 November – so suddenly that his wife, who had gone out to have her hair done, could not be summoned quickly enough to witness his last moments. Years earlier, Thurber had joked all too prophetically about his wife's frequent visits to a hairdresser: 'When I'm on my deathbed, Helen will be at the hairdresser's.'

VESPASIAN
(9–79)

An Emperor ought to die standing.
Suetonius, 'Vespasian', *Lives of the Caesars*
(written *ca* 120)

Titus Flavius Vespasianus became Roman emperor in 69 despite not only his fairly humble origins – his father and grandfather were both tax-collectors – but his disrespectful treatment of his awful predecessors. During Nero's song-recitals he used to leave the room or fall asleep, but although forced to spend some time in hiding from the Emperor's murderous wrath he was restored to favour. When Caligula blamed him for neglecting his duty of keeping the streets of Rome clean, surprisingly Vespasian suffered no worse punishment than having his gown stuffed full of mud. Wonderfully fortunate to survive these episodes, with the support of the army he came to power and reigned for ten years before dying of a fever on 23 June 79. According to the biographer Suetonius, he carried on with his imperial duties even while on his deathbed; then struggled to rise, muttering the words quoted above, and died in the arms of attendants.

Suetonius also records, as an example of Vespasian's renowned wit, a more famous comment made shortly before his death: '**Vae, puto deus fio [Oh dear, I think I am becoming a god**]'. This statement was truly prophetic, for Vespasian was deified immediately after his death – being the fourth Roman leader (after Caesar, Augustus, and Claudius) to be granted this honour.

During his reign, Vespasian stabilized the tottering government and economy of Rome, consolidated conquests in Britain and Germany, and began an ambitious building programme in Rome. He was often taxed with avarice, and on one occasion while serving as proconsul in Africa made himself unpopular enough to get pelted with turnips; but he lived modestly, usually treated his enemies and critics leniently, and showed a strong, often coarse, sense of humour. 'The dark unrelenting Tiberius, the furious Caligula, the feeble Claudius, the profligate and cruel Nero, the beastly Vitellius, and the timid, inhuman Domitian': the misdeeds of other emperors, thus memorably characterized by Edward Gibbon, have ensured their fame. The acts of decent Vespasian are virtually forgotten, except for one basic benefaction to mankind: his installation of public urinals in Rome is commemorated in the French word (*vespasienne*) for such a convenience.

Richard
WAGNER
(1813–1883)

My watch!
Ernest Newman, *The Life of Richard Wagner,*
Vol. IV (1947)

No thunder attended the twilight of a demigod on 13 February 1883; Wagner's last moments were desperately human.

In the early afternoon the composer was working in his study in palatial lodgings in Venice, where he had taken his family to escape the cold northern winter. Suddenly his bell rang twice, violently. The maid who answered the summons hurried back to Cosima, Wagner's wife, to report that he had been taken ill and had asked for 'The doctor and my wife'. Cosima found her husband racked by a spasm, apparently having ruptured a blood vessel in his heart. While she was helping him to a seat, his watch fell out of his pocket. '**My watch!**' he exclaimed.

It is ironic that Wagner's last expressed thought should refer to time, since one of the recurrent criticisms levelled against him as a composer and conductor was his failure to keep time. This was, in truth, no real failure, but a consequence of his scorn for a metronomically regular beat and his belief in the virtue of modifying tempi for expressive purposes. His watch was precious to him for another reason: it was a gift from Cosima. The illegitimate daughter of Franz Liszt, she had left her husband – Wagner's protégé and devotee, the conductor Hans von Bülow – for Wagner, whom she married in 1870. As he might have wished, he died in her arms; she lived on for almost fifty years, devotedly tending the sacred fire of the Wagnerian cult and directing the Bayreuth festivals.

Anton von
WEBERN
(1883–1945)

> I was shot... It's over.
> Hans Moldenhauer, *Anton von Webern* (1978)

The precise circumstances of the violent death of Webern, one of the most influential of twentieth-century composers, remained mysterious for several years and gave rise to many legends. Not until 1961, owing to the researches of the musicologist Hans Moldenhauer, were the bizarre facts made public.

At the end of March 1945, when Vienna was suffering from heavy air-raids and threatened by advancing Russian armies, Webern and his wife left the city to join members of their family in the mountain village of Mittersill, near Salzburg. There they remained quietly for several months after the war, while the place was occupied by United States troops.

On 15 September 1945, Webern went with his wife to spend the evening at the apartment of one of their daughters and her husband, Benno Mattel. Mattel, recently demobilized, was engaging in black-market activities. That evening he was visited by two American soldiers who, under the pretence of making an illegal deal with him, intended to incriminate and arrest him. While the soldiers were talking to Mattel in one room, Webern sat with his wife in another room; then he stepped out into the unlit hallway to smoke a cigar. There he apparently bumped into one of the soldiers, a cook named Raymond Bell, who, believing himself attacked, panicked and shot Webern three times in the stomach before running off for help. The composer staggered back into the room, uttered his final words, and died soon afterwards. At a subsequent military investigation Bell claimed that he acted in self-defence, not recognizing in the darkness that his

Webern

assailant was a small, emaciated, elderly man. Although the findings of the investigation are not known, presumably this plea was accepted; Bell died of alcoholism ten years later, haunted by guilty memories of his action.

Webern's mentor and great friend, Arnold Schoenberg, died on 13 July 1951. His last word, appropriately, was **'Harmony'**.

Select Bibliography

This list offers a selection of sources for unattributed statements in the text and of recommendations for further reading.

Addison
Peter Smithers, *The Life of Joseph Addison* (1954)

Agatha
Butler's Lives of the Saints, edited by H. Thurston and D. Attwater (1956)

Austen
W. and R. A. Austen-Leigh, *Jane Austen: Her Life and Letters* (1913)
John Halperin, *The Life of Jane Austen* (1984)

Beethoven
Maynard Solomon, *Beethoven* (1977)
Peter Latham, *Brahms* (1975)

Buckingham
M. A. Gibb, *Buckingham* (1935)
C. R. Cammell, *The Great Duke of Buckingham* (1939)
Hugh Ross Williamson, *George Villiers, First Duke of Buckingham* (1940)

Buddha
Alfred Foucher, *The Life of Buddha* (1963)
Hermann Oldenberg, *Buddha* (1882)

Burns
J. G. Lockhart, *The Life of Robert Burns* (1828)
F. B. Snyder, *The Life of Robert Burns* (1932)
R. T. Fitzhugh, *Robert Burns: The Man and the Poet* (1971)

Caesar
Michael Grant, *Julius Caesar* (1969)

Caligula
J. P. V. D. Balsdon, *The Emperor Gaius (Caligula)* (1934)

Select Bibliography

Carew
Sir William Monson, *Naval Tracts*, edited by M. Oppenheim (1902), Vol. II
Margaret Rule, article on the *Mary Rose* excavation, in *National Geographic*, May 1983

Caroline
Peter Quennell, *Caroline of England* (1939)
Charles Chenevix Trench, *George II* (1973)

Charles II
Raymond Crawfurd, *The Last Days of Charles II* (1909)
Maurice Ashley, *Charles II* (1971)

Chekhov
David Magarshack, *Chekhov* (1952)
Sophie Laffitte, *Chekhov* (1974)

Chesterfield
W. H. Craig, *Life of Lord Chesterfield* (1907)

Chopin
Selected Correspondence of Fryderyk Chopin, edited by A. Hedley (1962)
Adam Zamoyski, *Chopin* (1979)

Corbet
The Poems of Richard Corbet, edited by J. A. W. Bennett and H. R. Trevor-Roper (1955)

Cranmer
Jasper Ridley, *Thomas Cranmer* (1962)

Crazy Horse
Mari Sandoz, *Crazy Horse* (1955)

Descartes
Elizabeth S. Haldane, *Descartes* (1905)
J. R. Vrooman, *René Descartes* (1970)

Dickinson
Martha Dickinson Bianchi, *The Life and Letters of Emily Dickinson* (1924)
T. H. Johnson, *Emily Dickinson: An Interpretive Biography* (1955)

Select Bibliography

Diderot
Arthur M. Wilson, *Diderot* (1972)
Otis Fellows, *Diderot* (1977)

Disraeli
Robert Blake, *Disraeli* (1966)

Duncan
Irma Duncan and A. R. Macdougall, *Isadora Duncan's Russian Days* (1929)

Gainsborough
Geoffrey Williamson, *The Ingenious Mr. Gainsborough* (1972)

George V
Harold Nicolson, *George V* (1952)
Christopher Hibbert, *Edward VII* (1976)

Goethe
Richard Friedenthal, *Goethe: His Life and Times* (1965)

Gogol
V. Setchkarev, *Gogol* (1965)
Henri Troyat, *Gogol* (1974)

Goldsmith
R. M. Wardle, *Oliver Goldsmith* (1957)

Grenville
The Voyage of John Huyghen van Linschoten to the East Indies, edited by A. C. Burnell and P. A. Tiele, Vol. II (1885)
G. H. Bushnell, *Sir Richard Grenville* (1936)
A. L. Rowse, *Sir Richard Grenville of the Revenge* (1937)

Hadrian
Minor Latin Poets, edited by J. W. and A. M. Duff (1934)
S. Perowne, *Hadrian* (1960)
R. Syme, *Emperors and Biography* (1971)

Himmler
Willi Frischauer, *Himmler* (1953)

Select Bibliography

Housman
Maude M. Hawkins, *A. E. Housman* (1958)

Ibsen
Elizabeth Sprigge, *The Strange Life of August Strindberg* (1949)
V. J. McGill, *August Strindberg* (1930)

Johnson
W. Jackson Bate, *Samuel Johnson* (1978)
Johnsonian Miscellanies, edited by G. Birkbeck Hill (1897)

Keats
W. Jackson Bate, *John Keats* (1963)
Robert Gittings, *John Keats* (1968)

Kelly
Charles Osborne, *Ned Kelly* (1970)

Latimer
Allan G. Chester, *Hugh Latimer* (1954)
John Strype, *Ecclesiastical Memorials* (1721)

Lawrence
Acta Sanctorum (August, Vol. II)
Butler's Lives of the Saints, edited by H. Thurston and D. Attwater (1956)

Mary
H. F. M. Prescott, *Mary Tudor* (1953)

Molière
John Palmer, *Molière: His Life and Works* (1930)

Moore
Carola Oman, *Sir John Moore* (1953)

Mozart
C. Bär, *Mozart – Krankheit, Tod, Begräbnis* (1972)

Napoleon
Mabel Brookes, *St Helena Story* (1960)
W. M. Sloane, *The Life of Napoleon Bonaparte* (1939)

Nelson
T. O. Churchill, *The Life of Lord Viscount Nelson* (1808)

Select Bibliography

Nero
B. H. Warmington, *Nero, Reality and Legend* (1970)
Michael Grant, *Nero* (1973)

Perceval
Philip Treherne, *The Rt. Hon. Spencer Perceval* (1909)
Mollie Gillen, *Assassination of the Prime Minister* (1972)

Picasso
Pierre Daix, *La vie de peintre de Pablo Picasso* (1977)

Pitt
Philip W. Wilson, *William Pitt, the Younger* (1928)

Poe
Arthur Hobson Quinn, *Edgar Allan Poe* (1941)

Pope
Maynard Mack, *Alexander Pope: A Life* (1985)

Rabelais
Jean Plattard, *The Life of François Rabelais* (1930)
M. A. Screech, *Rabelais* (1979)

Rasputin
R. J. Minney, *Rasputin* (1972)

Rhodes
W. T. Stead, *The Last Will and Testament of Cecil John Rhodes* (1902)
Sir Thomas E. Fuller, *The Right Honourable Cecil John Rhodes* (1910)

Scott
P. Brent, *Captain Scott* (1974)
Elspeth Huxley, *Scott of the Antarctic* (1977)

Socrates
Editions of Plato's *Phaedo* by H. Williamson (1904), R. Hackforth (1955), and D. Gallop (1975)

Stein
Janet Hobhouse, *Everybody Who Was Anybody* (1975)

Sterne
Wilbur L. Cross, *The Life and Times of*

Select Bibliography

Laurence Sterne (1929)
David Thomson, *Wild Excursions* (1972)

Taki
John R. Black, *Young Japan* (1883)
Additional information provided by Professor Naotoshi Yamagishi, Nara University

Wagner
G. A. Hight, *Richard Wagner: A Critical Biography* (1925)

Webern
Hans Moldenhauer, *The Death of Anton Webern* (1961)
Willi Reich, *Schoenberg: A Critical Biography* (1971)

PN 6328 .L3

Exit lines

DATE DUE